INVADERS IN BRITAIN

BRIAN WILLIAMS

'In this year, the chieftain Cerdic and his son Cynric, came with five ships to Britain . . . and they fought against the Britons.'

Publication in this form copyright © Jarrold Publishing 2006.

Text copyright © Jarrold Publishing.

The moral right of the author has been asserted.

Series editor Angela Royston.

Edited by John McIlwain.

Designed by Simon Borrough

Picture research by Jan Kean.

The publisher wishes to thank John Rhodes for reading the text.

The photographs are reproduced by kind permission of: Aerofilms: 23t; AKG-Images: 86b; Alamy: 24l (Thislife Pictures), 61bl (Leslie Garland), 93 (Network Photographers); Ancient Art & Architecture Collection: 13tr, 21, 37t, 39l; Art Archive: 26tl, 34, 37b, 43b, 72b; Bodleian Library: 75t; Bridgeman Art Library: 19b (National Museum of Antiquities), 20cl (Ashmolean Museum), 20r (Biblioteque Municipale, France), 22tr, 23c (British Library), 24, 30tl (Dean & Chapter of Durham), 30br, 33br (Ashmolean Museum), 35tr (British Library), 44bl, 45t (Manchester City Art Gallery), 47 (British Library), 50t (British Library), 59tr (Ashmolean Museum), 68tr (British Library), 70tr (British Library), 70b, 75b (British Library), 77b (British Library), 83c, 84, 85b (Society of Apothecaries), 86tr, 89 both (Biblioteque Nationale); 68b (Burlington Paintings, London); Peter Brimacombe: 81r; British Library: 44tl, 46cl, 51c, 56tl, 57tr 79cr; British Museum: FCr, 27b, 32bl, 32r, 33tl, 35c, 43tr; Collections: 8 (Robert Estall), 15/16 (Roger Scruton), 16/17 (Ashley Cooper), 18 (Robert Hallman), 26b (Robert Estall), 29br (John D Beldom), 36 (Graeme Peacock), 41 (Frank Fitzpatrick), 48/49 (Simon Warner), 73tl (Dennis Barnes), 82 (Paul Watts); John Crook: 77c; Colin Dixon: 38tr, 39tr, 60tl; Geoff Doré: 7t, 51tr, 74b; Mary Evans: 59br, 85c, 88tl; Sonia Halliday: 22bl, 40b; Robert Harding: 10/11; English Heritage: 4 (Jonathan Bailey), 13b, 16t, 28tr, 71t, 83t (Jonathan Bailey); Epic Scotland: FCl; Michael Holford: 32tr, 44br, 52b, 57b, 60b, 61tr, 63 both, 64/65, 65 both, 66, 66/67, 68tl, 78, 79bl; Heritage Images: FCt, 5, 16bl (British Museum), 19t (British Museum), 27t, 28t (Colin Dixon), 40t (Museum of London), 43c, 56tr (British Museum), 73br; Imperial War Museum: 81tr, 91tr; Jarrold Publishing: 25br, 30bl, 31, 42, 58, 76, 80, 92b; Maidstone Museum & Bentlif Art Gallery: 92t; National Maritime Museum: 88/89; Popperfoto: 91bl, 94cr; Public Record Office: 74tr, 94tl; Rex Features: 90b, 93tr; Royal Armouries: 64cl, 71cr; Royal Collection © HM Queen Elizabeth II 2006: 87; Scala: 38b (Pierpont Morgan Library); Scotland in Focus: 11t; Mick Sharp: 9, 45br, 50bl; Sheffield Galleries & Museum Trust: 93c; Skyscan: 69; Michael J Stead: 29t, 72tr; TopFoto.co.uk: 7b, 14bl, 15tr, 49c; Topham Picturepoint: 90t; York Archaeological Trust: 52t, 53, 54 all, 55 all, 94b; Wales Tourist Board: 6; Werner Forman: 11b.

The quotations on pages 90 and 91 are copyright © Winston S. Churchill and are reproduced by permission of Curtis Brown Ltd, London, on behalf of The Estate of Sir Winston Churchill.

The artwork on page 14 was created by Roger Hutchins.

The maps were created by The Map Studio Ltd, Romsey, Hampshire.

A CIP catalogue for this book is available from the British Library.

Published by:
Jarrold Publishing
Healey House, Dene Road, Andover,
Hampshire, SP10 2AA
www.britguides.com

Set in Minion.
Printed in Singapore.

ISBN-10: 1-84165-166-4
ISBN-13: 978-1-84165-166-8   1/06

 Pitkin is an imprint of Jarrold Publishing, Norwich.

CONTENTS

INVADERS AND SETTLERS

'…this little world, this precious stone set in the silver sea, which serves it in the office of a wall, or as a moat defensive to a house, against the envy of less happier lands …'

John of Gaunt, in William Shakespeare's Richard II, *Act II, Scene i*

BRITAIN, SHAKESPEARE'S 'SEA-GIRT ISLE', has stood fortressed against invasion for thousands of years, guarded by its remoteness, its natural barriers and its insular inhabitants. Yet, over the centuries, conquerors considered it a tempting prize, and an even larger number of peaceful settlers have found it a desirable residence.

The first humans to make Britain their home wandered into it across dry land, for prehistoric 'Britain' was simply a coastal bulge on a much bigger land mass. Europe in the Ice Age was peopled by nomadic hunter-gatherers, and Britain's population probably numbered a few thousand at most. Then, about 8,000 years ago, the great ice sheets shrank. Sea levels rose, leaving Britain surrounded by water, an island group on the fringe of Europe. The seas that now washed these new shores served both as a defensive barrier and the only route to outside contact and adventure. Ships sailed in and out, to trade, to conquer and to move populations.

As each group of new settlers arrived in Britain, they set up communities with their own traditions and customs, often defending their lands tenaciously against subsequent newcomers. So invasion, or its threat, has been a recurring theme in British history. The first recorded confrontation began more than 2,000 years ago, when Celtic warriors galloped in their battle chariots to challenge Roman soldiers who were splashing ashore onto their land. The Romans came in ships across the Channel, led by their general, Julius Caesar.

MEDIEVAL MIGHT

Castles secured the Norman Conquest of 1066. Later castles, like 13th-century Caerphilly, were built as shows of force to tighten the grip of English kings on Wales.

Invaders in Britain focuses on the thousand years after Caesar's first landing, in 55 BC. Less than a century later, the Romans returned to conquer and reshape southern Britain as an imperial province. In the 5th century AD, there arrived the Anglo-Saxons, Germanic peoples who spoke new languages. From them, southern Britain gained a new name: England. Northern Britain, settled by Picts and Scots, also felt the impact of their arrival, while the people of Wales fought to maintain their distinctive ancient British language and culture.

In post-Roman Britain, warrior-chiefs strove to establish kingdoms, while missionaries carried their Christian gospel to the strongholds of paganism. From the 8th century, written records chronicle new threats from the North Sea, as Norwegian and Danish Vikings settled and raided the coasts of north and south. English, Irish, Scots and Welsh fought and mingled with these latest newcomers, who introduced yet more new influences on everyday life, law and language. And it was a descendant of Vikings, William of Normandy, who launched the most famous invasion of Britain – the Conquest of England in 1066. William's Norman dynasty introduced another cultural implant, the 'French connection' that reshaped much of medieval Britain.

After 1066, no invader managed to conquer Britain. English, Scots, Welsh and Irish fought, quarrelled and finally coexisted. Yet fear of invasion lingered for centuries after William the Conqueror. Kings looked uneasily abroad, generals built forts, politicians hatched alliances, while from beyond the seas an assortment of rebels, malcontents, would-be kings and disgruntled relatives lurked in exile. Most of these sought refuge with rival powers such as France, hoping to raise an invasion army and so topple their enemies.

Throughout the centuries, British coasts have been guarded against unfriendly incursion. Though the threat seldom resulted in full-scale attack, some of the invasion scares passed into national mythology: the Spanish Armada galleons massing in the Channel in 1588, the Jacobite march into England in 1745–46, Napoleon assembling his invasion barges in 1804, Hitler's *Luftwaffe* duelling with the Royal Air Force in 1940.

Defence against the foreign invader has taken various forms. The evidence is still to be seen: ancient hill forts in Wessex, Scottish brochs, Hadrian's Wall, medieval castles, squat Martello towers built to repel Napoleon, relics of the mighty Victorian Navy such as HMS *Warrior*, decaying concrete pill-boxes and air-force museums recalling the heroics of the Second World War. In the turbulent history of Britain, invasion has been an ever-present threat, its consequences and legacy often more surprising and enduring than those who fought for king and country on long-vanished battlefields could ever have foreseen.

REMINDERS OF NAPOLEON

The Martello tower at Aldeburgh in Suffolk is one of more than 100 such defences, reminders of an early 19th-century invasion scare when Napoleon Bonaparte contemplated a cross-Channel expedition to teach a lesson to the 'nation of shopkeepers'.

ANTI-PANZER PILLS

A concrete pillbox on the River Thames at Lechlade in Gloucestershire, designed to hold up invading German armour, and now a peaceful relic of Second World War invasion fears.

7

CHARIOTS AND COHORTS

THE ROMAN WALL

Hadrian's Wall (AD 122) is the most remarkable tribute to Roman military engineering. It extended 117 kilometres (73 miles), with troops stationed in mile castles at 1.6-kilometre (1-mile) intervals. It was a barrier to northern incursions, and an effective way to regulate cross-border movement.

THE ISLANDS off the north-west European mainland had been called 'Pretanic' by a voyager of 325 BC, and this name later evolved into the Roman 'Britannia'. To the Romans, the islands were remote and obscure. They found its weather unpleasant but Britain's crops, its minerals (especially tin) and even its weatherproof woollen cloaks were of value. The Romans also noted that the British bred good hunting dogs, but otherwise to them the islanders seemed of little significance.

The Britons were predominantly Celts, an ancient people rooted in central European history, whose tribal groups shared an inheritance of language, customs and culture. To the Romans, the Celts were barbarians, yet fascinating for their savage energy, skill in battle and strange customs. Bravery, boasting and a tendency to family quarrels were other Celtic attributes, along with heavy drinking and feasting, song and a love of decoration, seen in their personal ornament and metalwork. Tribal kingdoms held the power in the land: Brigantes, Catuvellauni, Atrebates, Coritani, Iceni, Durotriges, Belgae – often at war with one another. From contacts with their fellow Celts in Gaul (an area including modern France), rulers in Britain knew of the new military power spanning Europe, for Gaul had already fallen to the Roman fighting machine. And from their new province of Gaul, the Romans were close enough to study Britain minutely. They saw a prize that looked prosperous and winnable, a worthwhile addition to the Empire. First came Julius Caesar, to test the resolve of the inhabitants and assess whether glory might be quickly won. He did not stay, for his goals were set higher and elsewhere. There was Roman contact in the intervening years, including perhaps interference in local politics, but it was almost a century before the Romans returned in force, and their hitherto unsoldierly emperor, Claudius, sought a famous victory.

The Roman conquest following the AD 43 invasion was a triumph of military organization and seduction into 'civilized' ways. Within a century, despite some violent resistance, the southern British tribes had been 'Romanized', although the west and north remained outside Roman Britannia. The invaders made Britain part of the Roman-Christian world, their rule lasting peacefully and prosperously for almost 400 years, until Anglo-Saxons crossed the North Sea to open a new chapter in the invasion story.

SNUG AND DRY

Many Iron-Age people of pre-Roman Britain lived in round houses with thatched roofs. Most had some kind of fence or bank around them; in England and Wales, some people moved permanently into hilltop forts, defended by earth banks, ditches and palisades of wooden stakes. This reconstructed village is at Castell Henllys, near Newport in Pembrokeshire.

HILL FORT HEROICS

'The British call a stronghold any densely wooded spot fortified with a rampart and ditch …'

Julius Caesar, writing about his second expedition to Britain in 54 BC

DESPITE REPORTS FROM GAUL about Roman military might, the British Celts felt secure in their island – confident in their own prowess with sword and chariot, and in the impregnability of their hill forts. These earthwork strongholds, already old when Caesar first landed, gave safe shelter in times of war. Some, like Danebury Ring in Hampshire and Maiden Castle in Dorset, had grown into settlements, even ranking as 'towns' or *oppida* – the Latin name by which Caesar described places in Celtic Gaul that were larger than villages. Regional centres such as Camulodunum (modern Colchester) were often, though not always, tribal capitals.

Caesar's British campaigns secured him prestige in Rome and – as the chronicler of his own victories – an enduring place in the history books. He first arrived on the night of 25 August 55 BC, with 10,000 soldiers in 80 ships. The southern tribes of Britain massed to meet this intimidating fleet on the cliffs and beach near Walmer in Kent. The sight of war chariots churning up the shallows so daunted the Roman legionaries that at first they refused to leave their ships. When they did, they faced bloody resistance and made little progress. After four weeks, the Romans sailed back across the Channel to Gaul.

SCOTTISH BROCH
Although safe from Roman invaders, people in Scotland took shelter from other raiders inside brochs – stone towers up to 15 metres (45 feet) high. This broch is on the island of Mousa, off Shetland.

HILLTOP STRONGHOLD
Hill forts like this one at Malvern in Worcestershire still dominate the landscape after thousands of years.

Caesar came back in July the following year, with a force perhaps three times larger. This time he landed unopposed. His most formidable opponents, the Catuvellauni, retreated to their Hertfordshire tribal stronghold (probably Wheathampstead) north of the River Thames, dismayed by news that their jealous eastern rivals, the Trinovantes, had made a swift deal with the Romans. Without allies, the Catuvellauni fell back on their ancient hill fort and traditional Celtic heroism.

The Romans, experienced in siege tactics, were not to be intimidated by earthwork ramparts and wooden stockades, even when these were manned by blue-painted, near-naked 'barbarians' howling defiance. Bringing up catapults, they stormed the Catuvellauni hill fort from two sides. 'After a very brief resistance the enemy gave way … great quantities of cattle were found there, and many of the fugitives were overtaken and killed,' commented Caesar laconically. The defeated British king Cassivellaunus made peace, after which Caesar returned to Gaul to deal with local difficulties, and pursue his political ambitions in Rome.

From their hill forts, the warriors of Britain resumed their watch on the sea, and on one another. For the next 90 years, ships crossing the Channel carried conspirators, exiles and trade goods between Britain and the Roman world. Around AD 40, a British prince named Adminius, banished by his father King Cunobelinus, asked Rome's mad emperor Caligula to invade Britain. Nothing came of this, but after Caligula's death the new emperor, Claudius, revived his invasion plans. Hill fort heroism now faced an even more demanding test.

CYMBELINE'S COIN
This gold coin bears the name of Cunobelinus, king of the Catuvellauni – the 'Cymbeline' of Shakespeare's play. The power struggle between Catuvellauni and Atrebates leaders seriously undermined British resolve to fight off the Roman invaders.

ROMAN RESOLUTION

IN LATE SUMMER AD 43, Roman troopships landed in Kent. The invasion was hardly a surprise. Southern British rulers lived in the shadow of Rome, and used Roman power to further their petty feuds. King Verica of the Atrebates, ousted by Cunobelinus, was the latest British leader to seek imperial help in exacting revenge. Rome's new emperor, Claudius, realized that crushing Britain would deprive Gaul's freedom fighters of a refuge among sympathetic Celts, besides gaining a splendid imperial trophy.

Having at first been unchallenged, the Romans fought their first serious battle at the Medway. Special forces, 'Batavians [Dutch], able to swim in full armour', crossed the river and attacked the British chariot-horses, while legionary troops forded shallows farther along and fell on the British flank. The dash and courage of British warriors, their intimidating tattoos, blaring horns and screaming war-cries, failed before the disciplined butchery of Rome's legions.

The British commander, Caratacus, retreated north beyond the River Thames, while the Romans waited for their emperor to join them from Rome. After the tribal centre of Camulodunum (Colchester) had fallen, the middle-aged Claudius swayed past cheering troops on an elephant. Over 16 days he received the submission of 11 kings, then went back, having 'for the first time reduced trans-Oceanic barbarians under the power of the Roman people' (as an inscription in Rome modestly put it).

THE ROMAN INVASION

The likely route taken by Roman troops in AD 43. Their invasion force assembled on the coast of Belgium and northern France, having sailed down the Rhine (the 9th Legion came from Hungary). The Channel crossing was probably made at the narrowest point, the Pas de Calais.

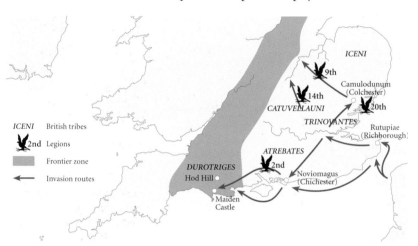

ICENI — British tribes
🦅 *2nd* — Legions
⬜ — Frontier zone
← — Invasion routes

ICENI
9th
14th
Camulodunum (Colchester)
20th
CATUVELLAUNI
TRINOVANTES
Rutupiae (Richborough)
ATREBATES
2nd
Noviomagus (Chichester)
DUROTRIGES
Hod Hill
Maiden Castle

'… when they [the Britons] did assemble, they would not come to close quarters … but took refuge in the swamps and forests … Plautius had a deal of trouble in searching them out …'

Dio Cassius, Greek historian, on the Roman invasion of AD 43

A LAND OF HEADHUNTERS

For the Celtic warrior, taking heads as war trophies may have had magical significance. The Romans, hardly squeamish, affected shock: **'When their enemies fall, they cut off their heads and fasten them about the necks of their horses …'**. Roman citizens read in horror that '… the heads of their most distinguished enemies they embalm in cedar oil, carefully preserve in a chest, and exhibit to strangers.'

'When you have all this, why do you envy us our poor hovels?'

Captive British leader Caratacus, viewing Rome's glories in the imperial capital

Caratacus rallied resistance, but in AD 52 he was betrayed by Queen Cartimandua of the northern Brigantes and taken as an honoured captive to Rome. The legions moved west and north, capturing hill forts and storming the Druid stronghold on the isle of Anglesey in Wales. The Iceni revolt (AD 60 – 61) led by the incensed Queen Boudicca was a final frenzy of southern resistance. Her hordes torched newly built London, but the Romans regrouped to win the decisive battle, after which the warrior-queen took her own life, rather than face capture.

The legions marched on, building forts and roads as they went. By AD 84, they were in Scotland, defeating Caledonian tribes at the battle of Mons Graupius. It was then time to consolidate. Hadrian's Wall (AD 122) and the Antonine Wall (AD 139– 40) drew frontiers within which the Romans were content to remain, imposing 'Roman peace' on their province of Britannia.

EMPEROR TRIUMPHANT

A coin of Claudius, minted in Britain. The emperor journeyed from Rome for a triumphant entry into the captured British stronghold of Camulodunum, today's Colchester.

INVASION BASE

Rutupiae (Richborough) in Kent was a beachhead for the Roman invasion. The port was later fortified as a Roman naval base to fight off Saxon raiders.

INVASION FORCE

WAR CHARIOT

Outmoded on the Continent, chariots were still used in battle by British Celts. Drivers raced about the battlefield, stopping to let their noble warrior leap off for death-or-glory combats.

STAB AND SLASH

The Roman short sword or gladius was a stabbing weapon, ideal for close-quarter infantry combat. Celts preferred a longer, slashing sword – also favoured by Roman cavalrymen. The Roman long sword or spatha eventually replaced the gladius.

THE ROMAN ARMY was the most efficient war machine of its day, and at its core was the infantry legion. Roman citizens to a man, legionaries served as assault troops and garrison guards, also forming the army's strategic reserve to crush incursion and insurrection. Furthermore, they were skilled engineers. On setting foot in enemy territory, they were trained to fortify a beachhead; on rapid marches across country, they built temporary night-camps to thwart surprise attacks; once victorious, they built stone-walled forts and military roads to secure their conquest.

MEN OF THE LEGIONS

Ten cohorts made up a legion of around 5,000 men. There were six 'centuries' to a cohort, each century (80 men) commanded by a centurion. Troops lived in eight-man sections, camping in goatskin tents and sharing rations. Each legion had some 120 cavalry troopers to act as messengers and scouts.

SHIELD TO SHIELD

Roman soldiers advanced behind a wall of curved shields. British fighters usually charged in a howling mass. The Romans kept close order, hurling javelins and stones, then rushed forward, thrusting with their short-bladed swords.

In AD 43, four legions, under Aulus Plautius, landed in Britain. These comprised some 24,000 men, backed by roughly the same number of auxiliaries (troops recruited from Roman provinces and border tribes). Auxiliaries, considered more expendable, went into battle first.

Legion commanders (legates) were normally Roman senators, while junior officers (tribunes) were often aspiring politicians. The legionaries were 25-year professionals, hardened by very tough training: long marches carrying packs, twice-daily weapons training, tree-felling, siege tactics, swimming, bridge construction and digging.

Each legion landed with 'mission specialists' – master builder, surveyor, catapult and arrow makers, boat builder, medical officers and orderlies. Present too were regimental priests or soothsayers, to invoke divine aid and advise the commander if the day was auspicious, or not, for victory.

PROFESSIONAL HEADGEAR

A Roman centurion's metal helmet, a little fancier but as functional as the helmets worn by lower ranks. Some Celts also wore helmets, which were more often made of leather.

BRITAIN DEFEATED

CITY THE ROMANS BUILT

Roman Silchester. Bottom right is the amphitheatre, and in the centre of town is the forum, the hub of municipal administration. Britain's next waves of invaders had little understanding of urban life, and such towns soon fell into ruins.

BURIED TREASURE

The Hoxne hoard of Roman silver was buried in Suffolk around 407, perhaps by an anxious householder fearful of invaders. It is now safe in the British Museum.

THE ROMANS HELD on to what they had conquered through a blend of military might and seductive cultural temptations. Much of Britain became 'Romanized', mingling Celtic and Roman traditions, religion and art.

From AD 375 Christianity was the imperial religion, evidence being found in wall paintings, mosaics and emblems. Villas, towns, baths and theatres symbolized the Roman 'good life' for those won over, though for hard-working country people and slaves life changed very little.

Southern Britain was 'Romanized' first, the west and north proving less amenable to change during the first hundred years of Roman conflict. The Brigantes of the north made a last stand near Scotch Corner, around AD 74. By AD 78, legionary

fortresses had been built at Caerleon and Chester, to complete the Roman hold on Wales, while another fortress at York sealed the invaders' grip on the north. Between AD 83 and 105, the legions campaigned in Scotland as far north as the Spey. Then in 122 Emperor Hadrian arrived on an inspection, and work began on constructing his wall, from the Tyne estuary in the east to the Solway Firth in the west. With the building of a second wall, the Antonine, further north, between the Firth of Forth and the Clyde, in 139–140, the Romans had secured their northern frontier. Northern Scotland was never subdued, nor did the Romans land in force on Irish soil.

Hadrian's Wall, held by generations of garrison troops, was to be breached by barbarians only four times in the next 250 years. By the 3rd century, more pressing problems came from the eastern sea, where pirates attacked settlements and disrupted trade. Roman-British defenders tried to keep these Germanic intruders at bay by building forts along the 'Saxon shore' of the south and east, and patrolling the coasts in a fleet of warships.

In 367 came a mass incursion into Roman Britain: Irish Gaels (called Scots by the Romans) and Picts from north of Hadrian's Wall, and Saxons and Franks from across the North Sea. The Roman garrison was weak, allowing the invaders a year-long orgy of plunder. Many villas were destroyed, their treasures looted. The occasional hoard of gold and silver, buried in haste by panicky householders, still comes to light after more than 1,500 years.

Three generals were sent in turn from Rome to regain control of the collapsing province. The third, Theodosius, managed to repel the pillagers and peace was restored, though not for long. In 383 another general, Maximus, ordered his best troops out of Britain to back his imperial ambitions. He was soon defeated, but the troops never returned. Thereafter, as Germanic tribes rampaged through neighbouring Gaul, Britain was virtually cut off from Rome. By 410, the last soldiers and officials were pulling out as Rome recalled its frontier forces. Emperor Honorius sent a last message: the British would have to defend themselves and their island against all comers.

HARDKNOTT CASTLE

Hardknott Castle (Mediobogdum) is an auxiliary fort high in the Lake District. It was built at the beginning of the 2nd century, during Hadrian's reign as emperor.

NORTHERN NEWCOMERS

SAXON SNARLER
A silver mount, with snarling animal head, inscribed with runes, probably from the scabbard of a Saxon seax, or short sword. From the weapon came the Saxons' name.

SAXON CHURCH BY THE SEA
St Peter's-on-the-Wall at Bradwell in Essex was built by St Cedd, Bishop of the East Saxons, in 654. It faces the sea on the wall of a Roman fortress.

ROMANS FACE PICTS
A slab from the Antonine Wall in Scotland, with a Roman cavalryman in battle with Pictish warriors. The Picts, who lived north of the Forth, were never Romanized.

AFTER ALMOST 400 YEARS of Roman rule, southern Britain was a land of opportunity for sea-borne newcomers. Regarded by the Roman-British as barbarians, this mixture of Angles, Saxons, Jutes, Frisians and Franks sailed in from the North Sea. People from the fringes of the Roman world, they were now eager for land and any rich pickings from the imperial carcass. Scots and Picts, traditional raiders, joined in the free-for-all.

As Rome crumbled, outlying territories like Britain were expendable. Local efforts to buy off, or drive off, the invaders failed. Estuary forts were all too easily bypassed by raiders. The newcomers simply took what they wanted. Some moved on for fresh plunder. Others settled among the ruins of what had been Roman Britain.

By the last years of the 6th century southern Britain was transforming into 'England' – land of the Angles, Saxons and their kinsfolk. The west (Cornwall and Wales) remained Celtic-British strongholds. Northern Britain too was reshaped, as Scots, Picts, British, Angles and Saxons jostled for land and dominance. A shifting pattern of kingdoms came into being, as first one warlord and then another claimed overlordship. The Britons had been largely Christian, and the faith held on in the north and west, nurtured and spread in Scotland and Ireland by missionary monks. In 597 a mission from Rome began the conversion of the newly settled and pagan 'English' in south Britain.

In the 9th century, Christian peace was shattered by a new wave of raiders from the sea. The sight of Viking longships spread panic, as rovers from Scandinavia ravaged the weaker kingdoms of Britain, settling wherever they were able. Norwegians chiefly targeted Ireland, Scotland, Wales and Cornwall, while Danes settled in the north and east of England. The Vikings brought turmoil and terror, but also a new infusion of cultural energy to Britian.

ANGLO-SAXONS MOVE IN

MUCH LATER, in the 9th century, the English recorded the stories of their arrival in *The Anglo-Saxon Chronicle*, a yearly summary of events. This history records that no Roman ruled in Britain after 410, and that in 446 'the British sent men over the sea to Rome and asked for help against the Picts, but they never had it. They sent then to the Angles'. An ill-judged move; when Roman Britain was beset by raiders eager for plunder, it was foolish to hire the raiders' kinsmen to defend the crumbling walls.

In 449, according to the *Chronicle*, warriors from three Germanic tribes came to Britain, in search of gold. These men – Saxons, Angles and Jutes – were willing to

FELLOWSHIP OF THE RINGS

Rings like this were given by Saxon lords to their followers, as tokens of the bond which existed between them.

FORTS OF THE SAXON SHORE

This map, originating from about 950, shows the Roman forts of the 'Saxon shore', built to guard the coast of Roman Britain against Saxon pirates.

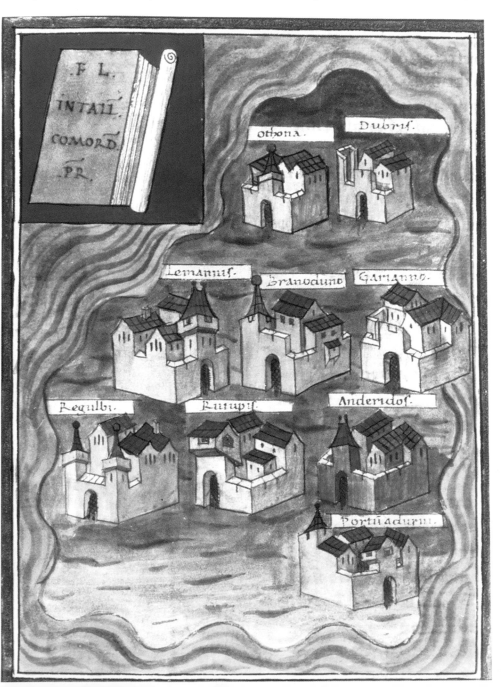

'Wondrous is this wall-stone. Ruined by fate, the fortresses have fallen; the work of giants is no more ... where in past times, many men ... shone in their war armour and looked on their treasures ... there the baths were hot in its centre.'

From The Ruin, *a Saxon poem about a ruined city, thought to be Roman Bath*

WARRIOR-KING'S HELMET

The fragmented helmet from the East Anglian ship-burial at Sutton Hoo. The nose, mouth, eyebrows and crest together form the shape of a bird. The leader who owned it died in the 600s.

fight anyone, for payment, and desperate British leaders hired them to keep out the 'barbarians'. Predictably, the mercenaries became greedy, asked for more, were denied, and began seizing land they had been paid to defend. The monk-historian Gildas, writing in the 540s, names Vortigern as the rash British king who in 449 invited two Jutes named Hengist and Horsa to defend him. There was a quarrel. Horsa was killed, but Hengist defeated the British and his son Aesc became king of a new Kentish kingdom. Whether or not this pair really existed, there must have been adventurers like them, opportunistic warriors who turned on their paymasters.

~

Defiant Britons rallied briefly around local leaders, one of whom was perhaps the prototype for the legendary King Arthur, but by the end of the 500s they held only the west, with one or two isolated kingdoms such as Strathclyde (south-west Scotland) and Elmet (Yorkshire). The invaders began calling the British 'foreigners' – *wealh* or *wylisc* ('Welsh' in modern English). The last major British 'resistance fighter' was Cadwallon, killed by Oswald of Northumbria in 633.

~

The Saxons (as it is simplest to call them, though they were a mixture of groups) set up their own kingdoms. Flooding in their homelands of north Germany and Denmark swelled the number of arrivals, as more and more families settled to a peaceful farming life. The historian Bede, writing in 731, tells us that Angles settled in East Anglia, the East Midlands and Northumbria; Saxons in Essex, Sussex, Middlesex and Wessex; and Jutes in East Kent, the Isle of Wight and Hampshire. The settlers left no contemporary written records, but archaeological evidence from graves broadly supports Bede's claims. Shunning the urban sophistication of Roman Britain, Saxons preferred village life. While they ploughed and sowed, the infrastructure of a once-rich Roman province began to crumble. Roads survived longest, while villas, baths and temples fell into ruin, walls were breached and their stones carted away, leaving roofless rooms inhabited only by nesting birds and mice.

ARTHUR THE KING

'The twelfth battle was on Mount Badon in which **960 men fell in one day from one attack by Arthur,** and no one overthrew them save him alone and in all the battles he was the victor.'

Nennius, Welsh historian c.800, *Historia Brittonum*

SO WHO LED BRITISH RESISTANCE to the Saxon and other invaders? Some stories credit Vortigern (the 'Over-King') with a degree of success in buying military aid to protect his realm, and Saxon settlement was usually by infiltration rather than mass invasion. But though evidence is slight, there does seem to have been British resistance on the battlefield. It was led first, from 460 to 475, by a shadowy figure named Ambrosius Aurelianus and then by a heroic warrior-king who in later tales became the focus for a legend of extraordinary richness: King Arthur.

CASTLE OF LEGEND

Tintagel in Cornwall – where Uther Pendragon had his secret tryst with Ygerna, and where, according to legend, Arthur was conceived. The castle remains are not much older than the 12th century, but evidence suggests the site was occupied 600 years earlier.

MOUNTED WARRIOR
This reconstructed detail, from the 7th-century helmet found at Sutton Hoo in Suffolk, shows a warrior on horseback charging down an enemy. The horse gave battlefield superiority.

Arthur presents a tantalizing puzzle: there are no eyewitness accounts, only stories and associations with places as far apart as the Eildon Hills in the north and Tintagel in the south west. Stories about him come from various sources, mostly much later, such as the medieval writers Geoffrey of Monmouth, Gerald of Wales and Thomas Malory. Their colourful mix of folklore, romance, religion and magic creates the Arthurian world of Camelot with its Round Table and gallant knights.

Nennius in his 9th-century *Historia Brittonum* lists 12 battles in which Arthur vanquished his enemies. We can only guess at how much truth lies behind such accounts. Did a Roman-British leader really organize an army of mounted, armoured warriors to defend his walled city? It is possible that, around 500, a war-leader, perhaps Arthur, won a decisive battle at 'Mons Badonicus' or Mount Badon – probably in the west, though the

BADBURY RINGS

Where Excalibur slew many? Badbury Rings near Wimborne in Dorset is one suggested site for the epic Battle of Mount Badon, where King Arthur wielded his sword Excalibur to such deadly effect.

BONDING TIME

Saxon lords entertained their warriors in the mead hall, feasting and telling tales of valour. In similar spirit, Arthur and his knights met at Camelot, bound by loyalty and comradeship.

'The leaders of the Britons assembled … in Silchester and suggested to Dubricius, Archbishop of the City of the Legions [Roman Caerleon] that, as their king, he should crown Arthur, son of Uther Pendragon.' Geoffrey of Monmouth, History of the Kings of Britain *(1135–50)*

site is unknown. Claimed locations for Arthur's last battle, Camlann, range from Cumbria to Cornwall, but the outcome is the same: destruction and the end of Camelot. The Arthurian myth became both a celebration and lament for a lost age of high promise, whether this was Roman Britain, the magic realm of Logres (a name derived from the Welsh name for England), or the golden age of medieval chivalry.

Perhaps through the post-Roman upheavals some Britons clung to the hope that the legions would return, or that some day a warrior-king with Christian virtues allied to Celtic magic would restore the golden age of villa and vineyard. The story of the 'once and future king' proved a potent combination of traditional warrior-myth and Christian hope that succeeding generations found irresistible. So Arthur was left sleeping, not dead.

CAMELOT: MYTH AND MAGIC ...

THE LOST KINGDOM

St Michael's Mount, near Penzance, Cornwall, was part of the magical kingdom of Lyonesse.

DEATH OF ARTHUR

Painted by Edward Burne-Jones in the 19th century, Arthur lies on his deathbed mourned by maidens.

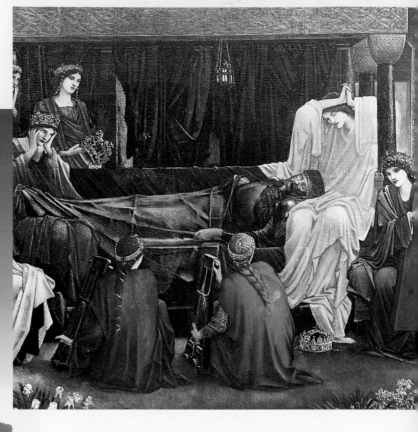

THE LEGENDS OF KING ARTHUR and his Knights of the Round Table are in a sense timeless. Tales have been countlessly retold of Arthur's magical sword Excalibur, the wiles of Merlin the magician, the love of Guinevere and Launcelot, and Sir Galahad's quest for the virtuous Holy Grail, the cup used at the Last Supper.

The stories inhabit the turbulent, twilight world of the fall of the Roman Empire. Barbarians are at the gates, and to save civilization there appears a hero with origins suitably magical. Arthur is said to have been born at Tintagel in Cornwall, his conception the result of a tryst between King Uther Pendragon and Ygerna, wife of Gorlois, aided by the sorcerer Merlin who transforms Uther into the likeness of Ygerna's husband. Fostered by the kindly old knight Ector, under Merlin's watchful eye, Arthur succeeds Uther as king at the age of 15, having dramatically drawn the sword from the stone – a feat no other could manage. He founds the fellowship of the

Battles
Birthplaces
Death or 'sleeping' places
Round Tables
Camelots
Merlin sites
Excalibur sites

Stirling
Eildon Hills
Drumelzier
Caledonian Wood
Bamburgh
Alnwick
Caerlaverock
Mote of Mark
Arthuret
Carlisle
Penrith
Richmond
Catterick
Derwent Water
Isle of Man
Wirral
Alderley Edge
Lincoln
Dinas Emrys
Lichfield
Bardsey Island
Preseli Hills
Dynevor
Brecon Beacons
Craig-y-Dinas
Swindon
Carmarthen
Caerleon
Liddington Fort
St Govan's Head
Dinas Powys
Bath
Brent Knoll
Salisbury Plain
Amesbury
Avalon
Winchester
Cadbury Castle
Old Sarum
Portsmouth
Tintagel
Badbury Rings
Dozmary Pool
St Michael's Mount
Lyonesse

ARTHURIAN BRITAIN

This map shows conjectural sites of battles and places connected with the legend of King Arthur.

AN ENDURING LUSTRE

'At the very south end of the church of South Cadbury stands Camelot,

sometime a famous town or castle .' So wrote the Tudor antiquary John Leland in 1542, on a scholarly mission for his master, Henry VIII. The Tudors were anxious to add Arthurian lustre to their own. Henry VII named his eldest son Arthur, and his second son Henry. That son, Henry VIII, had the 13th-century Round Table in Winchester Castle redecorated, with himself as Arthur.

Round Table, summoning brave knights from far and wide, and the Lady of the Lake gives him the special sword Excalibur (swords had magical virtues in Celtic and Germanic lore).

King Arthur and Queen Guinevere hold court at Camelot. Suggested sites for Camelot include Viroconium, a Roman city south-east of Shrewsbury; Caerleon on the River Usk in Wales, a Roman garrison fort; Tintagel; Winchester in Hampshire and Cadbury Hill in Somerset. At Camelot, the Round Table could seat 100 knights: '… their service equal and none before or after his comrade. Thus no man could boast that he was exalted above his fellow', according to *Le Roman De Brut* by Robert Wace, from about 1155.

Did Arthur die in his last battle? It is said that an army of British Romans sailed away, to settle in Gaul. Was its leader Arthur, referred to as 'Riothamus', a title probably meaning 'supreme king'? Other stories describe how Arthur, mortally wounded, is taken to Avalon – the Fortunate Isles or 'island of apples'. Glastonbury was suggested as the location for his tomb, but hard evidence is lacking. The medieval historian William of Malmesbury preferred the romantic legend that King Arthur was not dead, but sleeping, 'wherefore the ancient songs fable that he is yet to come'.

GLASTONBURY
Mystery, sanctity and legend surround the Somerset tor.

KINGDOMS COME

'In this year two chieftains, Cerdic and his son Cynric, came with five ships to Britain … and they fought against the Britons.'
The Anglo-Saxon Chronicle *for 495*

KING OF THE KENTISH MEN

Ethelbert of Kent was one of the first bretwaldas ('kings of all Britain'). His fame attracted the missionary Augustine from Rome, and he also laid down the first known Anglo-Saxon laws.

THE NEW ENGLISH KINGS were proud of their invading ancestry. The West Saxons of Wessex traced their line back to Cerdic and Cynric, sea-voyagers from north Germany or Denmark. Other English kingdoms also traced back their ruling dynasties to the chiefs of invading war bands, or even to the gods – placing Hengist and Horsa (the original Kentish mercenaries) alongside the Germanic god Woden at the root of their family tree. *The Anglo-Saxon Chronicle* goes even further in saying: 'from this Woden sprang all our royal families …'.

OFFA'S DYKE

King Offa of Mercia stamped his authority on his realm by building a great earthwork 'Offa's Dyke', still visible today. Offa's word was law across Mercia, Kent, Sussex and Wessex. He attacked the Welsh and, to hinder retaliation, built a barrier along his western border. Offa's Dyke was a ditch 2 metres (over 6 feet) deep, behind an earth bank three times that height, topped by a wooden palisade. The rampart stretched about 180 kilometres (112 miles) from the Dee to the Severn, and probably took ten years to construct.

OFFA'S DYKE

Built on the orders of King Offa of Mercia to mark the border between his realm and Wales, the earthwork originally had a wooden rampart along at least part of its length.

The English lived by a pagan heroic code, based on loyalty to their warrior-lord. The greatest of these local rulers claimed the title 'bretwalda' – ruler of Britain. Such overlords were Ethelbert of Kent (who received the Christian mission of Augustine in 597) and Raedwald of East Anglia, the possible 'Sutton Hoo king' (see pages 32–33). Early Saxon England was full of kings. Fighters foremost, they were strong enough to win and keep territory, and plunder, for their men. Tightly knit, closely related tribal groups chose their king (*cyning*, 'man of family') from leading warrior ranks. Kings ruled from barn-like wooden palaces, or halls, leading small armies of followers bound by the 'loyal unto death' code of Saxon warriors.

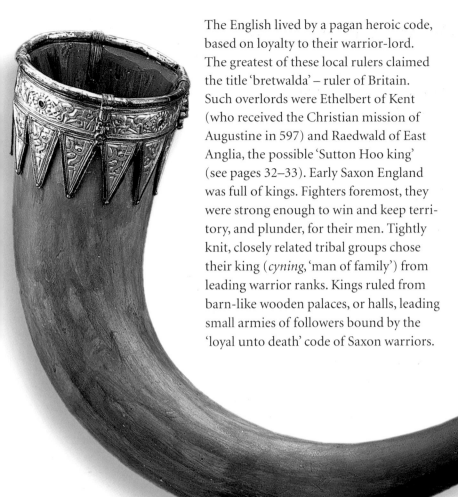

SAXON DRINKING HORN
Made from the horn of the extinct aurochs, or wild cattle, this 6th-century drinking vessel from a burial at Taplow in Buckinghamshire would have been used for feasts in a Saxon lord's great hall.

from its 6th-century Hampshire stronghold north to the Thames, east into Sussex and west up to the River Tamar in Devon.

In the north, Bernicia and Deira formed the kingdom of Northumbria, whose early kings – Edwin (reigned 616–33), Oswald (reigned 634–42) and Oswy (reigned 642–70) – ruled from great timbered halls such as that at Yeavering. Progressing around his kingdom, a king would stay in each hall once or twice a year, holding court to settle disputes, hunting by day and feasting at night, before moving on with his loyal retinue of followers. Such was the pattern of life for the new rulers of much of England. Though Mercia's remarkable King Offa (reigned 757–96) was the first to call himself 'king of the English', it was the royal line of Wessex that in time produced the kings who would rule a united land.

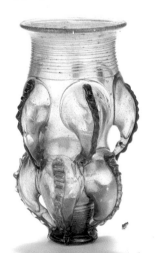

RHINELAND GLASS
A 5th-century glass claw-beaker, found in County Durham but made in the Rhineland. It could have belonged to a Roman-Briton, but rich Saxons also enjoyed fine tableware.

Frequent wars saw smaller kingdoms engulfed by larger ones. Kent, pre-eminent under King Ethelbert (reigned c.590–616), later came under the sway of Mercia and Wessex. Sussex, ruled by 'South Saxon' kings until 773, fell to Mercia and then Wessex. East Saxons in Essex, having absorbed the Middle Saxons (Middlesex) by 600, were taken over by Mercians. In the east was East Anglia, kingdom of the Angles, which covered Suffolk ('south people') and Norfolk ('north people'). From its Midlands heartland, Mercia expanded into the Thames valley and north to the Humber, while Wessex spread

THE NORTHLANDS

PICTISH BULL

A Pictish cross-slab from the 8th century. The Picts had a distinctive culture, seen in their stonework, but their language is now lost.

ROYAL PALACE

The palace at Yeavering in Northumbria, at the time of King Edwin. In the background is a 'grandstand' for people who are gathered to be baptized by the missionary Paulinus, and in the foreground is the Great Enclosure, for cattle. Reconstruction by Peter Dunn.

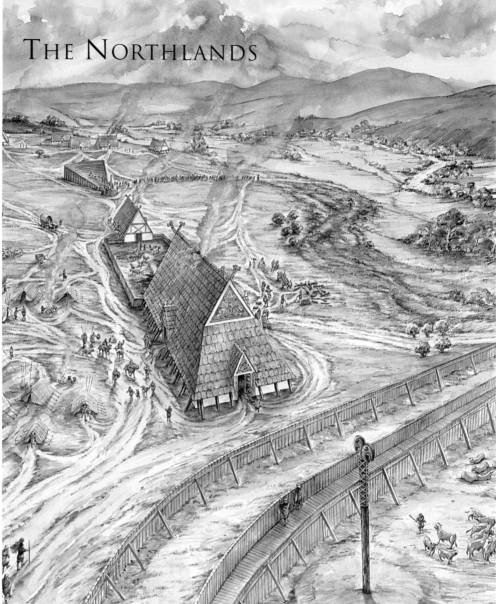

NORTHERN PATCHWORK

Scotland was not yet a kingdom. In fact northern Britain was tussled over by Picts, Scots, Britons and Angles, each of them defending their own territories.

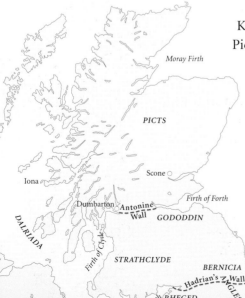

KINGS, WHETHER ENGLISH, British, Pictish or Scots, often ruled with ruthless ferocity. Ancient codes of honour demanded revenge for spilt blood, kindling frequent feuds and wars – yet the North preserved oases of religious calm and artistic achievement.

Caledonia (Scotland; Alba in Gaelic) was homeland to four main groups:

Picts, Scots, Britons and Angles. The Picts ruled from Orkney south to the Forth. Scots, from Ireland, controlled Dalriada (Argyll) in the west. Angles settled in Bernicia (Lothian), which became part of Northumbria; the Northumbrian king, Edwin, founded Edwinesburh (Edinburgh).

As the power of the Angles grew, Britons were pushed westward, holding on to Strathclyde, with their capital at Alcluyd (Dumbarton).

'*The very peoples of the English, their kingdoms and their kings, fight among themselves.*' *Alcuin (c.732–804), Northumbrian monk; adviser to Charlemagne*

Christianity did not end traditional blood-letting in north Britain. A typical tale of murder and mayhem saw King Edwin of Northumbria attacked in 626 by a would-be assassin from Wessex. In revenge, Edwin marched south, killing 'five kings there and a great number of people'. This made him the strongest king in England, until his defeat by Cadwallon of Gwynedd and Penda of Mercia in 633. Edwin's successor Oswald destroyed Cadwallon, but was then slain in 642 by Penda – who in 654 was killed in turn by Oswald's brother Oswy. And there were still Picts and Scots to fight as well!

In the far north, Picts and Scots eyed one another warily. 'Scotti' raiders, Celts led by sons of the Irish king Erc, had established their Scottish foothold around 500. Already converted to Christianity by St Patrick, they were united into one kingdom (Dalriada) by Columba. This shrewd churchman helped establish Aidan of Dalriada as a great king, and converted the Pictish king Brude from Druidism. The Picts had lived undisturbed for many years, north of the old Roman wall, and stoutly resisted all foreign incursions – in 685 they defeated the Angles in battle at Nechtansmere (Dunnichen in Angus), checking Northumbrian expansion. Pictish power seemed secure. However, the Pictish custom of matrilineal succession (through the mother's line) made unchallenged rule a rarity, and weakened their grip on an emergent 'Scotland'. The Scots of Dalriada chose kings through tanistry – succession by a previously elected member of the royal family. In 834, Alpin of the Scots and Eoghann of the Picts were together overwhelmed by an army of invading Vikings. Both kings died. After this calamity, one man claimed both crowns: Alpin's son, Kenneth MacAlpin (who had Pictish kinswomen). By 844 he ruled a united kingdom of Picts and Scots.

Warrior ferocity was fuelled by the oaths of loyalty sworn between kings and their followers at boisterous feasts in halls, where the deeds of dead warriors rang out in song. Ironically, despite the blood-letting, Northumbria was Britain's finest centre of scholarship, with its great monasteries at Monkwearmouth and Jarrow. Here saints and scholars preserved the best of Celtic, Christian and Classical influences, keeping alive literacy and literature in an age often described as 'dark'.

WORTH FIGHTING FOR

The Romans had never settled Scotland. From 500 to 850, local warlords and invaders competed for dominance, while Christian missionaries strove to win souls.

RUTHWELL CROSS

This cross in Dumfries and Galloway is a superb example of early Northumbrian-style Christian art. Its inscriptions include a runic quotation from an Old English Christian poem, The Dream of the Rood, *composed in the 8th century. Stone crosses may mark meeting places for worship where there was no church.*

SAINTS AND SCHOLARS

SAXONS AND VIKINGS lived in a world haunted by supernatural beings – giants, dwarves, witches, elves and trolls. Walking in fear of the unknown, they carried amulets or charms to ward off evil and sickness, and cast runes to seek signs. Their gods were those of the northlands: Woden (Odin), lord of magic and leader of the 'Wild Hunt'; the storm god Thunor (Thor); Tiw, god of glory, honour and warriors; and Frigg, goddess of childbirth.

The Britons displaced by Saxons had been largely Christian (since Roman times). Saintly missionaries such as Ninian, Patrick, Columba, Kentigern and Aidan spread the Celtic form of Christianity in the north. In the south, a mission from Rome arrived in Kent in 597, to tackle the pagan Saxons. Its leader Augustine, fearful of the Kentish men's terrifying reputation, nervously took his message to King Ethelbert. Afraid of witchcraft, the king insisted on an open-air meeting but afterwards allowed Augustine the use of an old Roman church in his capital. Ethelbert became a Christian; Augustine became the first Archbishop of Canterbury.

Raedwald of East Anglia, another cautious convert, permitted a Christian altar but only inside an older pagan temple. Christian bishops followed suit, often siting churches on pagan sites. When Ethelbert's daughter married Edwin of Northumbria, her Roman priest Paulinus completed a rapid conversion of the northern kingdom, becoming the first Archbishop of York. Yet Saxons were slow to give up their old traditions and on Edwin's death, Paulinus fled back to Kent. The Celtic church was loosely structured, with many priests working alone, though some authority resided in monasteries such as that founded by Columba at Iona and by Aidan at Lindisfarne. The Roman structure, imported by Augustine and his successors, was more centralized. There were disputes over various matters, including the date of Easter, and in 663 the Synod of Whitby was called to decide which tradition – Celtic or Roman – should be used. Rome won.

Monastic wealth was growing, especially in Northumbria, where energetic Church leaders included Cuthbert (*c.*625–87), Wilfrid (634–709), Benedict Biscop (*c.*628–89), and his pupil the Venerable Bede

SAINTLY RELICS

Part of St Cuthbert's coffin lid, and his pectoral cross, buried with him in 687 and eventually resting at Durham.

LICHFIELD'S LUKE

St Luke, from the 8th-century Lichfield Gospels, an illustrated manuscript exemplifying the high level of artistic achievement in Anglo-Saxon England.

MONASTIC HARMONY

St Paul's Church, Jarrow. Founded in the 680s by Northumbrian nobleman Benedict Biscop, the twin monasteries of St Paul's (on the Tyne) and St Peter's (on the Wear) were 'bound together in one spirit of peace and harmony' according to Bede, who was educated in them and went on to become the leading historian of his age.

(*c*.673–753), the historian who spent his life in the monasteries at Monkwearmouth and Jarrow. To Bede, we owe much of what is known as Saxon history.

By the time of King Ine of Wessex (reigned 688–726), Christianity was firmly rooted among English, Scots and Picts: as Ine's law put it, 'A child is to be baptized within 30 days; if it is not, 30 shillings' compensation is to be paid'.

When King Offa of Mercia died in 796 he was acclaimed a leader of European Christendom, a man to be reckoned with by both the Pope, the head of the Church in Rome and Charlemagne of the Franks, Europe's greatest king and soon to be crowned Holy Roman Emperor (nominal ruler of much of western Europe). Offa's English were for the most part Christian, like their neighbours in Ireland, Scotland and Wales, though not all were pious.

'Cuthbert … was wont to resort to those places and preach in such villages as were seated high among craggy, wild mountains … whose poverty and barbarity made them inaccessible to other teachers …' English historian Bede, on the strenuous missionary work of St Cuthbert

SUTTON HOO

THE SHIP REVEALED

The Sutton Hoo ship in 1939. Features of the burial suggest that the East Anglian royal family had once come from Sweden. The ship burial itself has echoes of Viking funerals.

SHOULDER CLASPS

This pair of clasps was made for a leather garment, and decorated with garnets and mosaic glass. The gold pin slipped through hinges to lock the two halves of the clasp together.

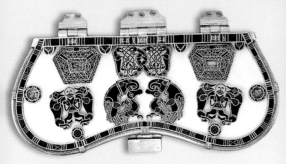

This purse-lid had a base of bone or ivory set into a gold frame with hinges to hang the purse by a strap from a belt. The decoration includes fine mosaic glass and garnets from Afghanistan. The leather purse, long decayed, would have contained gold coins.

A ROYAL BURIAL

Death rites for the hero of *Beowulf*, the Old English epic poem, have clear parallels with Sutton Hoo: 'The people ... then raised a high, broad barrow on the cliff; it could be seen from afar by seafarers; in ten days they built the beacon of the bold warrior ... **they laid rings and jewels in the barrow** ... they let the earth keep the treasure of the earls, the gold in the ground ...'.

BESIDE THE RIVER DEBEN near Woodbridge in Suffolk lies a group of low mounds, first documented in 1601, but far older. Despite the efforts of tomb robbers, these ancient burial sites preserved their most astonishing secret until 1938. Mrs Edith Pretty, owner of the land, asked local archaeologist Basil Brown to investigate. The first three mounds yielded bones, fragments of stone and metal, and evidence of a ship burial. In 1939, digging began on the largest mound.

As war clouds darkened that summer, Brown made one of the 20th century's major archaeological finds. Preserved in the sandy soil was the outline of a wooden ship which, it transpired, had been buried in the early 600s. Nearly 30 metres (98 feet) long and 4.2 metres (14 feet) at its widest, this ancient rowing boat had been dragged uphill to a burial ground and laid in a trench. A chamber within had probably held the body of a great warrior-king, though no traces of it remained. Who was he? The most likely member of the East Anglian royal dynasty was King Raedwald. Coins found on the site were dated to 625–30, and Raedwald died in 624 or 625.

Among the remarkable royal artefacts and treasures buried with him were a bronze cauldron, a silver dish, drinking cups, folded textiles, leather shoes, silver buckles, a lyre, a sceptre, an Egyptian-style bronze bowl and regal war gear – an iron sword, spears, mail shirt and a magnificent iron helmet. Ship burial with such 'grave goods' was an ancient pagan rite, though Christian items too were found: it seems that the dead king, perhaps like Raedwald a Christian convert, had never entirely renounced the old religion.

Mrs Pretty generously gave the Sutton Hoo treasures to the nation and most are now in the British Museum. The grave field, with its grassy mounds, remains emotive for visitors. With a leap of imagination, they can picture the scene over 1,300 years ago, as East Anglians dragged a wooden boat to the hilltop and laid their king to rest with ritual splendour.

Detail of the ceremonial 'whetstone', or sceptre, with a bronze stag motif, from Sutton Hoo.

HEROES AND HISTORY

IN THE SAXON WORLD, the warrior was hero, in fact and fiction. He carried a wooden shield and wore an iron helmet. Body-armour, such as a mail coat, was seldom worn. Favourite Saxon weapons were the sword and spear, and later the long-handled axe. Spears, thrust from behind the protection of a wooden shield or hurled like javelins, were up to 2 metres (6 ½ feet) long.

The most prized weapon was a sword, crafted with patient skill by iron-smiths, using a technique known as pattern welding to twist iron rods together. This produced a herringbone pattern on a two-edged blade about a metre (3 ¼ feet) long. The sword was sheathed in a wooden scabbard lined with sheep's wool and covered with leather. A good sword was passed from father to son.

MONASTIC CHRONICLES

Year by year, monk-chroniclers recorded the past events that had shaped Britain: 'This year [501] Port and his two sons Bieda and Maegla came to Britain with two ships, at a place which is called Portsmouth ... **This year [509] Saint Benedict the abbot, father of all monks, went to heaven.'**

LINDISFARNE ARTISTRY

A brilliant abstract-design page from the Lindisfarne Gospels (7th–8th century), which display a fusion of Celtic, Classical and Byzantine elements typical of Saxon-age Christian art.

Few Saxons were literate. Monk-scholars guarding monastic libraries wrote down the deeds of kings and bishops in chronicles, but most history was passed on orally. Story-poems were sung by minstrels called scops, who plucked a harp or lyre while reciting the words. Performances like this occur in *Beowulf*, most famous of all Saxon poems, which, though written down around AD 1000, was composed centuries earlier, possibly between 700 and 750, and describes events in early 6th-century Scandinavia. Story-poems mingled history and heroics, like the sagas of Germanic/Norse tradition, about sea voyages, monsters, gold, greed, battles, darkness and death. There are war poems, Christian poems such as *The Dream of the Rood* (Cross) and sad poems of exile. Saxon poetry does not rhyme, but is rich in descriptive phrases (a boat becomes a 'foamy-necked floater', for instance) and is driven along by alliteration.

As well as Latin and Old English dialects, Saxons also wrote in 'secret letters' called runes – marks of mystery and power used for inscriptions, spells, riddles and charms. 'Sing that same charm into the man's mouth and into both his ears and into the wound before he puts on the salve' are runic directions for use with a herbal healing paste mixed from old soap, apple juice, egg and ashes.

SCRIBE AT WORK

A 12th-century picture of a scholar-monk, possibly Bede, the 'venerable' and most illustrious Saxon historian.

THE HELMET

The most famous Sutton Hoo object is the helmet. This is a steel replica, made by the armourers of the Tower of London. The original (see page 21) was iron, covered in tinned-bronze foil.

'The iron blade was adorned with deadly, twig-like patterning, tempered with battle blood … the ancient treasure, the razor-sharp ornamented sword …'

From Beowulf (c.1000), the greatest poem in Old English

35

THE VIKINGS IN BRITAIN

HOLY ISLAND

The monastic settlement of Lindisfarne on Holy Island, Northumberland, was twice ravaged by Vikings. Stones from the priory were used in the 16th century to build the castle, overlooking the sea.

DESTRUCTION RECALLED

Viking vandals stomp across the 9th/10th-century Lindisfarne Stone, possibly a depiction of the raid of 793 that so shocked Saxon England.

NO DITCH OR DYKE, nor so mighty a king as Offa, could protect a long coastline from predatory invaders who came in ships. In 789, while Offa was negotiating the marriage of his daughter to the Emperor Charlemagne's son, news came of a minor outrage: three Norwegian Viking ships had landed in Dorset. The local official, taking the visitors for traders, had ridden from Dorchester to meet them in the king's name … and was promptly killed.

In 793 came a more drastic calamity, as Vikings struck again. This time they attacked one of the land's most holy places, the monastery founded by Aidan in Northumbria: 'heathen men miserably destroyed God's church on Lindisfarne, with plunder and slaughter', in the words of *The Anglo-Saxon Chronicle*. Iona was raided in 802, destroyed in 804.

These first onslaughts caused great alarm. From Charlemagne's court in Europe, the English scholar Alcuin of York wrote to King Ethelred of Northumbria, expressing horror: 'Never before has such terror appeared in Britain as we have now suffered.' Alcuin attributed the raids to God's judgement for people's sins.

Vikings voyaged far from their homes in Norway, Sweden and Denmark, driven by lack of good farmland to seek new lands to settle. Norwegians chiefly targeted Ireland, Scotland, Wales and Cornwall, while Danes headed for north and east England. Where unresisted, they founded settlements based on farming, fishing and trading. Against rich, fertile kingdoms strong enough to retaliate, they engaged in sporadic warfare, culminating in a sustained mass attack on south-east England in the mid 800s.

The Viking invaders, matching the Saxons for seamanship and courage in battle, proved durable and adaptable. Like the Saxons before them, they were also after land. Most exchanged raiding for settlement and, from the Shetlands to East Anglia, began forging new nations with new linguistic and cultural qualities.

OSEBERG SHIP
Found in Norway in 1904, this Viking ship was used for a royal burial around 850.

LONGSHIPS LAND

MOBILITY WAS THE KEY to Viking success. Their ships were stout enough to sail across the North Sea, but so shallow they could be rowed up most British rivers. Raiders usually managed to land, fight and sail away before the locals could rally forces to defeat them. Viking traders could roam wherever they wished, from Iceland to the Mediterranean, and Viking migrants seeking new settlements took to the sea in vessels able to carry women, children, household goods and farm animals.

Known as 'longships', as opposed to the stubbier cargo ships of the time, Viking warships were clinker-built (oak planks were overlapped to form the hull). They were slender, open-hulled boats over

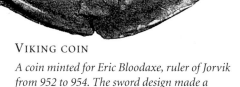

VIKING COIN

A coin minted for Eric Bloodaxe, ruler of Jorvik from 952 to 954. The sword design made a defiant statement.

20 metres (65 feet) in length and about 5 metres (16 feet) in the beam. Crews manned long oars when there was too little wind to fill the single, square sail – 15 pairs of oars propelled the average craft, though the biggest fighting ships or *drakkars* may have had 60 oars and such ships must have been well over 45 metres (150 feet) long. Ferocious dragons' heads glared from up-curved prows, and from the mast tops ' the gold shone like fire in the sun', according to a Scandinavian poet. Weather vanes, often gilded, were a useful aid to a sailing skipper. The ship was guided by a broad-bladed steering oar, fastened to the right or 'starboard' (steerboard) side at the stern.

FAR-RANGING NORSE WAVE-RIDERS

Viking longships were equally at home on the open sea or a shallow estuary. Every man aboard was a muscular oarsman, as well as a warrior.

Seafarers navigated by ocean currents, sun, stars and their knowledge of coastal landmarks, rocks and sandbanks.

No part of the British Isles was safe. Norwegian Vikings sailed to the Shetlands and Orkney Islands, where the Jarlshof settlement provides evidence of the small communities they established in the 800s. Longships also landed on the Isle of Man, which remained Norwegian until 1266.

Other Viking ships ranged west to Ireland where, after first landing in 795, the Vikings founded settlements at Dublin, Wexford and Waterford. They traded as well as raided, with slaves among their merchandise, many of them Picts captured along the coasts of Scotland.

The longship seamen had much in common with the Saxons they fought. They wore similar clothes – thick trousers and tunics for men, long dresses for women, with leather shoes, and woollen or fur cloaks for winter. They spoke a related language, and shared a common heritage of pagan deities, traditional beliefs in spells and charms and the power of runes. Their songs and stories echoed the same heroic deeds. Their social and family structures were very similar, as were their homes and farms.

In battle, Vikings wielded similar weapons to their foes: swords (which, as with the Saxons, were often passed down from father to son), spears and axes. Though he could ride a horse, a Viking usually fought on foot, hand-to-hand, until he or his enemy dropped.

FIERCER THAN HE LOOKS

Real-life Vikings scared their enemies. This slightly more docile stone image from Yorkshire (10th-century) shows a helmeted warrior with spear, sword, axe and shield.

WAR HELMET

This Viking-age helmet from York has cheek flaps and chain-mail neck guard.

VIKINGS ON THE MARCH

'THERE WAS WARFARE AND SORROW over England,' says *The Anglo-Saxon Chronicle*, but the 9th-century Viking attacks affected all realms, north, south, east and west, in the still disunited kingdom. Viking warriors earned a fearsome reputation, particularly the famed *berserkers* who, clad in bearskins, were supposedly inspired by the gods and gifted with manic strength as they 'went berserk'. Their code held that the best death for any Viking was in battle, for the belief was that chosen warriors were borne to Odin's heavenly hall of Valhalla, to fight all day and carouse all night.

In 839 an army of Norwegian Vikings defeated the Picts, killing many of their best warriors. By the 870s, longships were in Strathclyde, landing an army that for four months besieged the British fortress on Dumbarton Rock. In the face of attack from overseas, some opportunists seized the chance to gain domestic advantage. Rhodri Mawr, king of Gwynedd in Wales, and Kenneth MacAlpin, king of the West Scots in Argyll, did not just fight the Vikings: they also gobbled up weaker neighbours, so furthering the unification of fragmented realms.

Raiders attacking England came mainly from Denmark. At first invading groups were small – perhaps 50 ships at most. In the 830s, Danish Vikings raided the Isle of Sheppey in Kent, skirmished along the south coast (Southampton, Portland) and attacked East Anglia. In 850–51 Danes camped for the winter in Thanet – a sign that local opposition was weak. Also in 851, a fleet of 350 Viking ships sailed into the Thames; the English, without a navy,

WEAPONS OF TERROR

Viking spears and axes had no unique killing power, but the invaders' rapid attacks and ferocity spread panic.

NO CITY WAS SAFE

Canterbury was attacked in 1011 by Vikings who murdered the archbishop when he refused to agree to a ransom deal. This 13th-century window in the cathedral commemorates the siege of the city.

could not stop such an army landing, and the Vikings duly sacked London and Canterbury. At this stage, their prime motivation was still 'loot' (such as coins, gold and slaves).

In 865, the biggest Danish army yet seen landed in East Anglia, apparently set on conquest and settlement, as well as plunder. Their leaders, an assortment of self-styled kings and earls, included Ivar 'the Boneless' with his brothers Healfdene (Halfdan) and Hubba (Ubbe), sons of the redoubtable Ragnar Lothbrok ('leather breeches' or 'shaggybreeks'). Rampaging into Mercia, the invaders scorned its feeble king's offer of gold for peace, then took horse for Northumbria, wreaking fresh havoc among the monasteries and churches, isolated and undefended. Whitby was ravaged and York captured.

Ragnar's sons had a score to settle with Northumbria's ruler Aella, who they believed had killed their father (by tossing him into a snake pit). In panic, Aella patched up his quarrel with King Osbert, whose throne he had usurped; it did no good – both were slaughtered by the invaders. In 869, Anglia's Christian king Edmund was defeated and horrifically slain when he refused to abandon his faith. He was later venerated as a martyr, his burial place becoming known as Bury St Edmunds.

Three English kingdoms had now fallen to the invaders. Only one – Wessex – remained free from Viking rule. The South West held the key to England's future and here one English leader, a son of Wessex, was destined for greatness. His name was Alfred.

BRITONS' STRONGHOLD
Dumbarton Rock, west of modern Glasgow, was the capital of the Britons of Strathclyde, whose kingdom fell to the Vikings in 870–71. The name comes from the Gaelic Dunbreatan *('fort of the Britons').*

Alfred Holds Fast

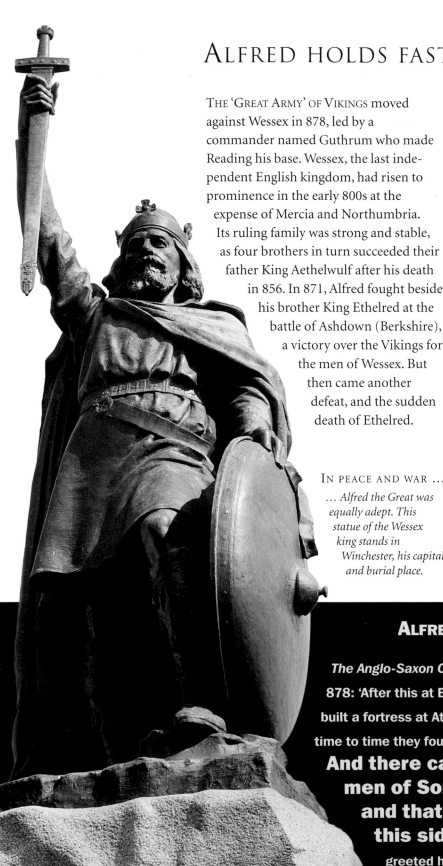

The 'Great Army' of Vikings moved against Wessex in 878, led by a commander named Guthrum who made Reading his base. Wessex, the last independent English kingdom, had risen to prominence in the early 800s at the expense of Mercia and Northumbria. Its ruling family was strong and stable, as four brothers in turn succeeded their father King Aethelwulf after his death in 856. In 871, Alfred fought beside his brother King Ethelred at the battle of Ashdown (Berkshire), a victory over the Vikings for the men of Wessex. But then came another defeat, and the sudden death of Ethelred.

Alfred, aged around 22, with a wife and young son, became king. He had to leave his brother's funeral to carry on the fight, lost again, and sued for peace. In 876, the war began again. Unlike the Vikings, Wessex men stopped fighting at harvest and winter time, and by 878 Guthrum controlled much of Wessex. Alfred was forced to seek refuge in the Athelney marshes of Somerset. The king's emergence from that low point was decisive. Rallying more Saxon leaders to his dragon standard, his defeat of the Vikings below Salisbury Plain at Edington (Wiltshire) in 878 was crucial. By the treaty of Wedmore following this battle, Alfred secured his own territory. The Vikings withdrew, by stages, to East Anglia, and Guthrum became a Christian – with Alfred as his baptismal sponsor.

Alfred was content to let the Vikings settle in the so-called Danelaw (roughly east of a line from Chester to London), with Guthrum as their king. His heartland of Wessex secure for the present, Alfred was

In peace and war …

… Alfred the Great was equally adept. This statue of the Wessex king stands in Winchester, his capital and burial place.

ALFRED RALLIES THE TROOPS

The Anglo-Saxon Chronicle records the English rally of 878: 'After this at Easter King Alfred with a small band built a fortress at Athelney, and from this fortress … from time to time they fought against the army [the Vikings] … **And there came to meet him all the men of Somerset and Wiltshire and that part of Hampshire on this side of the sea** … and they greeted him warmly.'

able to capture London (886) and, by marrying his daughter Aethelflaed to Ethelred, ealdorman of Mercia, gained a useful ally. Energetically, he reorganized his defences by creating a network of fortified towns, called *burhs* (boroughs). He also built the Wessex *fyrd* (militia) into a rapid reaction force (half tilling the fields at home, while half stood armed and ready), and ordered large ships with many rowers to patrol the south and east coast, ready to fight off Viking longships at sea.

Viking attacks renewed after Guthrum died in 890. In 892–93, yet another 'great army of Danes' (as the English called them) appeared off Kent in a fleet of 250 ships, 'horses and all', having ravaged Frankish territory from Paris to Brittany. As more ships landed in the Thames, Alfred called up his allies and took to the field. The campaign ranged from Devon to the north until 897, when the Viking army broke up, 'those who were moneyless' (according to the *Chronicle*) taking ship back to France.

FAMILY TREASURES

Gold rings belonging to Aethelwulf of Wessex, father of King Alfred, and his daughter Aethelswith, queen of Mercia.

RECORDED FOR POSTERITY

Part of The Anglo-Saxon Chronicle, *written in Old English, describing Alfred's defeat of the Vikings at Edington, Wiltshire, in 878.*

'ALFRED HAD ME MADE'

The Alfred Jewel, so inscribed, was found near Athelney in Somerset, where King Alfred took refuge from the Vikings. The jewel may have been part of a bookmarker, sent by the king as a gift.

THE WARRIOR CODE

'Do not leave your weapons at home when working in the fields; you never know when you might need your spear.' — Viking saying

THOUGH SAXONS AND VIKINGS had to work hard to feed themselves, fighting was seldom far from their thoughts. The two peoples had much in common. Each came from northern European origins. Their pagan gods were much the same (Viking Odin was Saxon Woden, for example). They were superstitious, fearful of evil spirits lurking in bog and fen. They loved songs and sagas in which heroes battled against hideous monsters; what better way to spend an evening in the lord's hall than to hear a poet recount the brave deeds of dead heroes? Such an evening might well end riotously, after hearty drinking with rowdy jests, impromptu trials of strength, wrestling and singing bawdy songs.

This society was based on a code of honour, kinship and loyalty. Warriors shared the spoils of victory, but willingly died for their lord and, once their leader had fallen, thought it shameful to leave the battlefield unscathed. Fleeing foes were slaughtered, to exact vengeance for slain comrades. Even in peacetime, blood feuds were common. In Saxon England, every man knew his own worth or *wer-gild* ('man-tax') – the compensation payable to his family if someone killed him.

Early Saxon war-bands, of the kind that landed to raid Roman Britain, were small – a fleet of five ships might land only 200 or so men, and a king's troop was unlikely to exceed 50. Similarly, early Viking raids were on a small scale, though as they gained a foothold in England, their armies grew larger. A Viking army had many kings and *jarls* (lords), and no single general to command it.

SAXON SPEARMAN

The iron-tipped ash spear was a favourite Saxon weapon for throwing and close combat.

SWORD-LORE

Swords were prized by fighting men and a good sword was thought to be imbued with magical qualities. Shown here are a 9th-century Saxon sword (left) and a slightly later Viking weapon. Both have silver hilts – precious weapons indeed.

Bands of Vikings traipsed after their own trusted leader, who was often the captain of the ship that brought them across the North Sea.

Saxons and Vikings rode horses, though almost always dismounted to fight on foot in battles that were bloody hand-to-hand trials of stamina, lasting until one side either fled or was slaughtered. The famous encounter described in the poem *The Battle of Maldon* shows how the warrior code could get in the way of sensible strategy. In 991 a band of East Saxons led by Earl Byrhtnoth marched to throw out Vikings landing on the River Blackwater in Essex. With foolhardy bravado, or outmoded gallantry, the earl did not fall upon the Vikings in their island camp, but allowed them to cross a causeway to open ground. He delivered a stirring address to his men; the Viking leader replied with an offer of a truce (for gold). The earl retorted that the only tribute offered to the invaders would be 'poisonous spears and ancient swords'. Formalities over, the fighting began. The English lost, but the poet praises Byrhtnoth for his noble hero-ism. He dies looking to heaven, his body-guards slain beside him.

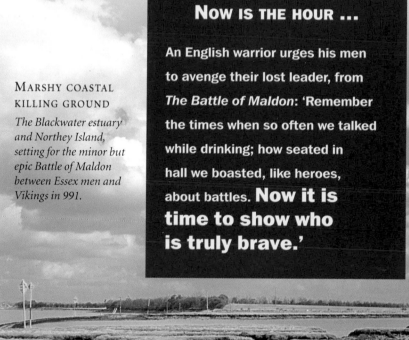

MARSHY COASTAL KILLING GROUND

The Blackwater estuary and Northey Island, setting for the minor but epic Battle of Maldon between Essex men and Vikings in 991.

NOW IS THE HOUR ...

An English warrior urges his men to avenge their lost leader, from *The Battle of Maldon*: 'Remember the times when so often we talked while drinking; how seated in hall we boasted, like heroes, about battles. **Now it is time to show who is truly brave.**'

45

FORGING THE NATIONS

A CHANGING MAP

During the time of early Viking invasions and later settlement, no one ruler was strong enough to rule all Wales or all England. There were a good number of kingdoms and settlement areas, but Wessex in the South West was the rising power.

ALFRED'S GRANDSON

Athelstan, king of England from 924 to 939, defeated an alliance of enemies at Brunanburh (Burnswark in Dumfries and Galloway), forcing King Constantine III of Alba (Scotland) to submit. This 14th-century illustration shows Athelstan, Alfred's grandson, secure on his throne as the 'great king' of Britain, with a European reputation.

'AND THREE SCOTS CAME to King Alfred in a boat without any oars from Ireland … because they desired for the love of God to be in a state of pilgrimage …'. So says the *Chronicle* for 891. Having crossed the sea in a skin boat with food for seven days, the pilgrims landed in Cornwall before hurrying inland to see Alfred – such was the reputation of this great king of the English.

Alfred had come to terms with the settlers occupying the Danelaw, which became a Scandinavian territory within Britain, with a permanent legacy of place names and law. But the rest of England was moving towards unity, based on Wessex.

Alfred himself referred to his land as Angelcynn, 'land of the English folk'. By encouraging education, he tried to repair the damage inflicted by constant warfare, and laid the foundations for a flowering of Saxon culture. His code of laws, adopting from custom 'those which seemed to me most just', gave equal justice to English and Viking alike and dealt with such energy-sapping matters as traditional blood feuds. Alfred's vision was of a nation united by military victory, yet upheld by faith and learning. When he died in 899, a new England was forming.

English expansion continued under Alfred's successors: Edward (reigned

'Every man shall provide two well-mounted men for every plough …'

From the laws of King Athelstan, on military service

899–925) and his sister Aethelflaed ('Lady of the Mercians'), Athelstan (reigned 925–39) and Edgar (reigned 959–75). Athelstan's victory at Brunanburh, over Scots, Welsh and Irish Vikings, made him the great king in Britain, and in 959 Edgar confirmed Saxon supremacy by accepting homage from Welsh and Scottish kings. Edgar's reign is often seen as the peak of Saxon achievement, with his kingdom extending north beyond the Viking stronghold of Jorvik (York). Jorvik itself remained an independent base for Viking trade, with its own kings until 954, and the aggressive Olaf Guthrisson (reigned 939–41) maintained the Viking tradition of raiding, north and south.

Wales felt under increasing pressure from English kings, who demanded tribute and employed military muscle to get it. Small border kingdoms such as Powys were all but absorbed into England during the 9th century, while other mini-states were subsumed into larger Welsh kingdoms, notably Glywysing (later Morgannwg) in the south and the western kingdoms of Dyfed and Gwynedd. Western Welsh kings such as Rhodri Mawr (died 878) made it their business to extend their influence at the expense of weaker neighbours. English rulers much admired Hywel Dda ('the Good'), who died in 950, for his success as a unifier and law-maker in Wales.

Welsh rulers were also kept busy fighting Viking marauders. Sailing the coasts of Wales on their trade routes between Ireland and England, the Norsemen were always ready to pounce on an undefended target. Settlements on the Welsh coast seem to have been few, but churches in Wales (at St Davids, for instance), like their English counterparts, did not escape Viking predators.

JUSTICE FOR ALL

The king, whether Scots, English, Welsh or Viking, administered justice, advised on law-making by a council of churchmen and nobles. In England, the ruling council was known as the witan.

THE MAKING OF SCOTLAND

ARRIVING VIKINGS upset the precarious balance which had existed in the North between Picts, British, Scots and English. Norwegian Vikings had begun settling Orkney and Shetland in the early 9th century, and later the western isles too. To all intents and purposes, Orkney was treated as part of Scandinavia.

Picts suffered most from Viking incursions, and their embattled weakness was exploited by Scots moving eastwards along the Great Glen towards the Moray Firth, a traditional Pictish stronghold. Scots fought the Norwegians when they met them in the north-eastern highlands, and several Scots kings were killed during invasions of Viking-held Moray. The big gainer in these tussles was Kenneth MacAlpin (died 859), who took advantage of failing Pictish power and English distraction (the Angles of north-east England had their own Vikings to worry about). MacAlpin pushed south into the lowlands to attack Strathclyde and Cumbria, creating a new royal dynasty with its capital at Dunkeld, in former Pictish territory. By about 900, Picts and Scots acknowledged the same king, and the united kingdom of 'Scotland' was known as Alba.

Most of MacAlpin's heirs met violent deaths either in battle or at the hands of rivals. In order to ease fears of his own overthrow, Constantine II made a power-sharing agreement with his cousin, whose son, Malcolm, succeeded Constantine as King of Alba. After Malcolm died fighting the English in 954, Constantine's son, Indulf, managed to capture Edinburgh from the English before he too was slain. Squeezed between Scots to the north and Viking Jorvik to the south, the northern English must have felt isolated. So too

SCOTS ON THE UP

Scotland about AD 1000. Scots kings gained power and territory through fighting Picts to the north and Celtic-British and English to the west and south.

'So from that spring whence comfort seem'd to come, discomfort swells. Mark, King of Scotland, mark ...'

William Shakespeare, Macbeth, *Act I, Scene ii*

did the Celtic-British in their last stronghold of Strathclyde; by the early 1000s, this kingdom too had fallen to the Scots, who had pushed their border as far south as the River Tweed.

Malcolm II (reigned 1005–34), king of Scots, was able to defeat both English and British, enhancing Alba's prestige and power. He was succeeded by his grandson Duncan, remembered from Shakespeare's 'Scottish play' as the Duncan murdered by Macbeth. Macbeth held the throne from 1040–57, ruling well apparently, until he shared the fate of so many Scottish kings, being killed by a vengeance-seeker.

Macbeth's nemesis was Malcolm III, known as 'Canmore' or 'big chief' ('top gun' might be a snappy modern translation). Malcolm had sought refuge in England from his enemies, and made allies too among the Vikings. As a result, his was a reign of new influences; his first wife was Scandinavian and his second, English – the saintly young Queen Margaret, who brought English customs and piety to Scotland. Malcolm gifted land to his Viking allies, who in return introduced a fresh infusion of Scandinavian language and culture to the south and east. Their language combined with British and English speech to create what became the dialect of Lowland Scots.

STONE OF DESTINY

Lia Fail, the Stone of Destiny, was used in the coronation of Scottish and Pictish kings. The stone was moved from Dunkeld to Scone in the 800s. There it remained until taken by Edward I of England to London in the late 1200s. Since its return to Scotland in 1996, the Stone has been in Edinburgh Castle.

HOLY IONA

Here St Columba founded a monastery in 563, and here eight Viking kings and many Scots kings were buried. The island once had 360 stone crosses; only three of these remain, dating from the 9th, 10th and 15th centuries.

From fury to farming

Every day another job

The Aelfric Pentateuch manuscript illustrated biblical scenes with drawings of Saxon peasants at work; from St Augustine's Church, Canterbury.

An Englishman's home ...

... was no castle, but in Saxon times a house of wood with walls of wattle and daub (woven sticks plastered with mud). This example is reconstructed at West Stow Saxon village in Suffolk.

Viking invasion left a legacy of settlement in Britain, from the northern isles to the flat lands of East Anglia. Most Norse newcomers settled down to farm, living in small villages, ploughing long, narrow strips of land ('furlongs'), using teams of up to eight oxen. Freemen (known as ceorls in Saxon England) often shared the work in cooperatives. Law and order was dispensed by their lord, whose land was measured in so many 'hides' (farm holdings).

The Vikings had shaken much of Britain – kingdoms destroyed, churches damaged, books burned. Even after many Vikings became Christian, their neighbours still shuddered at tales of horrific pagan torture such as that reputedly inflicted on King Edmund of East Anglia. Yet for most people, life passed peacefully from season to season, following the demands of the farming year. Whatever their origin, the peoples of the British Isles had much in common because most depended on similar methods of farming for their livelihood.

Farmers felled woodland to clear fields, which they ploughed in strips using a simple ard (scratch plough) and a heavier ox plough with a mould-board that could turn heavy clay. A villager's home, wood-framed with wattle walls and straw-thatched roof, was usually crowded, with three generations commonly living together. Inside, a fire burned for warmth and cooking, its smoke filtering out through thatched roof and eaves. Candles of tallow (animal fat) might flicker in the gloom, but most Saxons regarded sunset as bedtime.

Families kept sheep for meat and wool; cattle and pigs for meat, hides and other useful items such as horn or bristle. Summer's harvest yielded wheat and rye for bread, barley for brewing ale and oats for animal feed and porridge. Meals might be bread, cheese, butter and buttermilk, milk, eggs, wild game – and a treat of roast pork when the family pig was butchered. Fish bones found by modern archaeologists in early refuse pits show that people enjoyed a wide variety of species: perch, pike, trout, herring, salmon and eels, as well as oysters, mussels and cockles.

OLD ENGLISH INTERIOR DESIGN
Like this reconstruction at West Stow, few houses had windows or much furniture apart from a wooden chest, beds, stools and perhaps a small table, with clay pots, iron cauldrons, and barrels for storage.

From grave remains and manuscript illustrations, it appears that some people of the time were tall – women's skeletons commonly measure 1.7 metres (5 feet 8 inches) and men's up to 1.8 metres (around 6 feet). Women wore their hair long, tied or plaited, while finds of razors suggest that some men shaved their chins, although most of them grew moustaches.

SLOW BUT SURE
Oxen were used to haul two-wheeled carts, which had to be robust to cope with the rough tracks that served as roads.

FRUIT AND VEG

People grew purple carrots, parsnips, small cabbages, peas, beans, onions and leeks, and collected wild roots such as burdock. Honey, for sweetening, was brewed into a potent drink called mead. Apples were grown for cider, or eating, along with plums, cherries and berries.

VIKING BRITAIN

BALTIC BAUBLES

Amber was a favourite material for jewellery, like this necklace. The fossilized tree resin was also fashioned into pendants and rings.

VIKING TREASURE

The Cuerdale hoard from Lancashire, a collection of Viking silver, includes more than 7,000 coins from Britain and further afield.

BY THE LATE 900s, Saxons, Scots and Vikings had established an uneasy relationship, based on similar lifestyles, a good deal of mutual suspicion, and a policy of 'deterrence'. English and Scots kings kept wary eyes on Viking farmers who might toss aside hoes and spades, and dust off swords and axes to join a newly landed band of Norse raiders. Most stayed peaceful. In eastern England, many Vikings who settled in what became known as the Danelaw took English wives, but kept their own language and customs. Although Saxon law prevailed over most of England, the Danelaw remained Scandinavian; here units of land were the 'wapentake' and not the English 'hundred', and freemen retained a bond to their lord rather than to the land.

Viking farmers often took over lands abandoned by Saxons, Picts or Scots. They ploughed and sowed the strip fields, kept slaves to help with heavy work, and traded with neighbouring communities. Viking women enjoyed considerable freedom, running the home while husbands were away on trading voyages or fighting. Women also attended the Althing, the law-making assembly where all freemen were allowed to have a say. On the Isle of Man, which was settled by Norwegian Vikings, the Court of

Tynwald is still elected from 'sheadings', or ship districts, into which the island was divided by the settlers.

Viking settlers gave new names to the places they occupied. Shelton (Yorkshire), for instance, became Skelton (easier for Vikings to pronounce). Many new names were given, often ending in '-by' (a suffix meaning any settlement, from a town to a farmstead). Holtby was the town by the wood, Moreby the town by the moor, and so on. Slingsby was named after a local whose nickname 'Sleng' apparently meant 'lazybones'.

WEIGHED IN THE BALANCE

Viking traders carried a set of balance scales and lead weights to check the worth of customers' coins. Most coins were 'clipped' (trimmed) to steal the gold or silver from them.

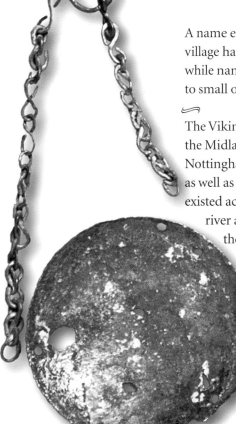

A name ending '-thwaite' means that a village had been cleared from woodland, while names ending in '-thorpe' were given to small offshoots from an older settlement.

The Vikings maintained military bases in the Midlands and the East, at Leicester, Nottingham, Derby, Stamford and Lincoln, as well as York (Jorvik). A flourishing trade existed across country by packhorse and river and then across the Irish Sea to the Viking settlement in Dublin. Towns within the Danelaw, such as Peterborough, Ely, Cambridge and Norwich, prospered. And none more so than Jorvik, a fortified city since Roman times, which by AD 1000 was the biggest and most bustling trading centre in Viking Britain.

DRESSED TO KILL

Viking women in Britain at first wore 'old-fashioned' long dresses with short sleeves, held in by a cloth wrapped around under the arms. Most adopted the long-sleeved dress and tunic favoured by Saxon women, and began covering their heads with headdresses and silk caps tied with ribbons. Brooches fastened the tunic's shoulder straps, and were also used to hang keys or household utensils from thongs or chains. Viking and Saxon men wore linen shirts, sleeved tunics and trousers, a cloak of fur or thick woollen cloth, with a belt for a knife or sword.

JORVIK

FACE OF A VIKING
A hard-working citizen of Jorvik, his features reconstructed from a Viking-age skull, using modern laser-scan technology.

WHEN IN 866 VIKINGS captured Eoforwic (York), the Northumbrian capital, they found it still bearing the marks of the Roman world – the walls, fortress and streets of a Roman garrison-city. Under Norse rule, the population, probably less than 2,000 before, grew five times that size, making Viking Jorvik one of the few cities in Britain worthy of the title.

Settlement of the north by invaders from the Great Army began in the 870s, when the Viking leader Healfdene (Halfdan) 'shared out the land of the Northumbrians' among his followers. 'Jorvik' (its new Viking name) became a bustling royal capital. The city had a cathedral (from around 627) and its kings were Christian – though still with traditional Viking tendencies. There was a thriving trade with Viking Dublin across the sea, as well as with smaller towns in England, such as Leicester, Derby, Lincoln and Stamford. Merchants travelled overland and along the rivers Foss, Ouse and Humber to Jorvik's busy waterfront and workshop quarters.

New streets of the time testify to this hustle and bustle. Coppergate takes its name from the local trade (*koppari* = cup-maker, *gata* = street in Old Norse). Metalworkers made all kinds of useful items: folding knives, nails, bolts, brackets, hasps, chains, hooks, locks, candle holders, spoons and fishhooks – as well as the essential arrowheads, spears and swords. There were coin-stampers, jewellers working stone, jet and amber from the Baltic, glassmakers, makers of cheap wooden cups and bowls, weavers and dyers, tanners and cobblers, comb-makers transforming red deer antlers into hair-combs, and people who could fashion a goose's leg bone into a whistle. Viking trade links extended astonishingly far. Pottery came to Jorvik from Germany, whetstones from Norway, silk from the eastern Mediterranean, an Islamic dirham (coin) from Uzbekistan, a cowrie shell from the Red Sea.

Cesspit remains show that Jorvik bread, made from wheat and rye flour, also contained weed seeds (such as corncockle) which would have made the bread not only very brown, but also potentially gut-wrenching. Vegetable remains are scanty (scrawny carrots and cabbages); herbs and fruit (apples, plums, cherries, sloes) are more plentiful. Butchers provided pork, beef and mutton as well as game. People used pottery jars for storage and cooking, wooden plates for eating off, and wooden cups for swilling down beer and wine.

After Jorvik's last king, Eric Bloodaxe, was expelled and killed near Barnard Castle in 954, the city's ruling jarls (earls) came under English control. At the Norman Conquest a century later, York, which was second only to London in wealth, still retained much of its distinctive Norse independence.

BEADS AND SHELL MONEY
Amber beads (top left) and this cowrie shell, from the seas around the Arabian peninsula, show how far-ranging was the trade from Viking Jorvik.

STEPPING OUT
A Viking shoe. Soft leather from cattle, deer or goat hide was sewn onto a sole cut from wood or hardened leather, and fastened with straps and buckles.

FACE TO FACE WITH A VIKING
Visitors to the Jorvik Viking Centre come face to face with the reconstructed Eric Bloodaxe, last Viking king of York.

REDISCOVERING JORVIK

Modern interest in Viking York began in the 19th century, but was stimulated by city centre redevelopment in the 1970s. Work at Coppergate, on the site of an old sweet factory, started in 1976. Since then, archaeologists have uncovered a rich assortment of tools and household items well-preserved in the peaty soil, as well as the pattern of streets with house-plots 5.5 metres (18 feet) wide. The Jorvik Centre, recreating life in Coppergate in 948, opened in 1984.

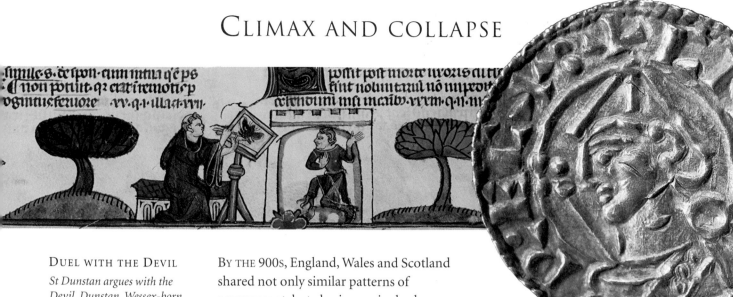

DUEL WITH THE DEVIL

St Dunstan argues with the Devil. Dunstan, Wessex-born archbishop, religious reformer and missionary, crowned Edgar King of England in 959, and was the king's most learned adviser.

COIN OF CNUT

Cnut held by ability an empire larger than any previous king of England. Neither of his vicious sons were of the same stamp.

BY THE 900S, England, Wales and Scotland shared not only similar patterns of government, but also increasingly close links, through trade, military adventure and, less brutal, royal ties and diplomacy. English kings ruled through a council, the *witan*, a group of nobles and churchmen who advised on new laws and taxes. The court of King Edgar at Winchester was among the most admired in Europe. But his was the last flourish. A Saxon 'golden age' ended in 978 with the murder of Edgar's son Edward, and the accession of Ethelred II, known as the Unready (from Old English *unraed*, 'evil advice').

Sensing weakness, Vikings launched fresh attacks. Ethelred's response was to buy off the marauders with gold (the so-called 'Danegeld') and grants of land. When this policy failed, he ordered a massacre within the Danelaw that incited a furious King Sweyn to invade with an army from Denmark. Ethelred fled to Normandy. He returned on Sweyn's death in 1014, but was defeated by Sweyn's vengeful son, Cnut, who had ambitions of his own.

On Ethelred's death in 1016, his son Edmund Ironside took on Cnut's army, only to die months after winning a share of the disputed kingdom. This left Cnut in possession of all England – he later added Norway to his realm. Cnut reigned until 1035, restoring peace and the submission of Welsh and Scots. When absent abroad, he entrusted England to its three most powerful earls: Leofric of Mercia, Siward of Northumbria and Godwin of Wessex. An already tense political situation was

HARD TIMES ...

... as recorded in *The Anglo-Saxon Chronicle*: '1053 ... This year ... the whole midwinter there was much wind ... and it was decreed that Rees, the Welsh king's brother, should be slain because he had done harm and his head was brought to Gloucester ... **And the same year Godwin the earl died, and Harold his son succeeded to the earldom.** 1054 ... This year went Siward the earl [of Northumbria] with a great army into Scotland, and made much slaughter ... In this year died Leo [IX] the holy pope ... and there was so great a murrain [disease] among cattle as no man remembered for many years before.'

complicated by dynastic rivalry. Cnut had married Ethelred's queen, Emma (a Norman), and their son Edward duly reigned after Cnut's older sons (Harold I and Harthacnut). With his accession, Danish rule in England ended, for Edward was more Norman than Saxon or Viking. His religious piety earned him the title of 'Confessor', and he devoted much energy to the building of Westminster Abbey, but he was no soldier and, crucially, his marriage to the daughter of Earl Godwin (the real power in England) produced no heir.

A confrontation loomed. Godwin's ambitions centred on his son, Harold, a capable war-leader who inherited the earldom of Wessex on his father's death in 1053. Harold slid into pole position as the popular candidate to succeed King Edward. But in both Scandinavia and Normandy, rivals were waiting to thwart his intent. The scene was set for a dynastic showdown.

HERE WE STAND

A group of Saxons seem to be contemplating an uncertain future, as shadows fall across their 'golden age' in England.

DEATH OF THE CONFESSOR

The deathbed of Edward the Confessor (top) in January 1066 and his burial the next day in his new church at Westminster, as depicted in the Bayeux Tapestry.

ELY CATHEDRAL

Founded as a monastery in 673 by Queen Etheldreda of the East Angles, Ely was rebuilt by Abbot Simeon, a relative of William the Conqueror, in 1093.

SAXON RULE ENDED in England on 14 October 1066, when King Harold II lost his life at the Battle of Hastings. Here surely was a turning point in history, when a crown almost saved through dogged resistance was then lost by impetuosity and exhaustion. And yet, though the nation had a new king, speaking a different language, there was continuity too – as there had been through all the previous invasions in Britain's history.

England's new master was William, Duke of Normandy, whose descendants were destined to reign in England long after their own duchy in France had been lost. The Norman invasion, the most famous in England's history, proved hugely significant for its people, especially those highly placed in the aristocracy and Church. It also affected the evolving nations of Welsh, Scots and Irish, since Norman ambition soon reached beyond the borders of England. Wherever it spread, Norman rule left a lasting legacy, in stone and statute.

Many have wondered what might have followed had Harold, not William, won at Hastings. English kings might have kept closer links with Scandinavia, rather than embarking on a centuries-long involvement with France. England and Scotland may have grown more like Sweden or Norway. Instead, the Normans turned England – and Britain – firmly towards 'the Continent' of mainland Europe, and in particular France.

Normans, invariably pictured grim-faced, are seldom viewed sympathetically – unlike their Viking forebears, whose past image as horn-helmeted pillagers and rapists has been softened by modern historians who stress their trading and settlement achievements. The Normans' most obvious testament took the form of castles and churches, massive and enduring, for the invaders were builders as well as soldiers. They added a monumental new layer to a growing edifice of nationhood based on foundations laid down by earlier invaders: Viking, Saxon and Roman.

BEST FOOT FORWARD

An iron stirrup, probably dating from the time of the Norman Conquest. Stirrups held mounted knights firm in the saddle.

MAILED MIGHT

A Norman cavalryman with lance and kite-shaped shield. William the Conqueror made certain that his invasion force had plenty of horses, for battle and for mobility between battles.

RIVALS FOR A CROWN

A coin of Harold II, bearing the profile of the king who fulfilled his father's hopes, but for a brief reign only.

THE SEAT OF KINGS

This picture from the Bayeux Tapestry shows Harold on the throne, while a courtier presents the sword of state. Stigand, the Archbishop of Canterbury, is on the right.

ENGLAND WAS UNEASY in the winter of 1065–66. By January, its weak and unpopular king, Edward the Confessor, was dead, leaving no son and heir. He had filled his court with officials from his mother's homeland, Normandy. With relief, if a degree of trepidation, most English earls threw their weight behind a leader they knew, Harold Godwinson. Harold was proclaimed king by the council of England and crowned in Westminster Abbey.

On his coronation day, 6 January 1066, Harold must have felt reasonably secure. He had swiftly and decisively exerted the wealth and power of the Godwin family (in 1052 he had returned from exile to reclaim the family lands after Edward had banished the Godwins for defying royal authority). He was a renowned soldier, commanding the loyalty of England's warlords. Above all, he held the crown. There were, however, two other claimants.

The first was Harald Hardrada, King of Norway, with ambitions to be a second Cnut. Born some five years before Harold, in 1015, Hardrada became king of Norway in 1045 with a European-wide reputation, gained fighting for the Byzantine Emperor Michael IV. He had survived battles in

60

Scandinavia, Sicily and Bulgaria; exile in Russia (he had married a princess of Kiev); and spent years trying to win the throne of Denmark from King Sweyn II. In the British Isles, he already ruled the Orkneys, Shetlands and Hebrides.

The other claimant was Duke William of Normandy. He too had Norse connections, since Normandy took its name from Vikings ('Norsemen') who settled there in 911. The bastard son of Duke Robert of Normandy and Arlette of Falaise, daughter either of a tanner or an undertaker (accounts vary), William had inherited the dukedom at the age of seven. Normandy was no place for a boy-ruler, and he escaped assassination more than once during brutal civil wars. Life had made him a tough soldier and astute politician, ruthless at seeing off all rivals – and seizing an opportunity.

William claimed that around 1051 Edward the Confessor had promised him the English throne, should Edward die childless. On his deathbed, Edward had assigned the kingdom to Harold: but could one believe such a dying wish? William thought not. And he held another diplomatic card: in 1064, during a journey to France, Harold had the misfortune to fall into William's hands. There was a show of amity: the Bayeux Tapestry represents Harold lending a hand in a punitive raid against one of William's enemies. While detained in Normandy, Harold had been persuaded, or tricked (he said), into swearing to help William claim the throne. Harold later repudiated his oath as having been made under duress; but it helped secure William the backing of the Pope, who sent a banner to show his support for the duke's claim.

As the winter of 1066 gave way to spring, contestants watched and waited, preparing for a three-cornered struggle which would decide who ruled England.

UNWELCOME TIDINGS STITCHED IN WOOL

A messenger brings news to Duke William. The Normans were well informed about Harold's actions and movements, as this scene from the Bayeux Tapestry shows. The tapestry, now in Bayeux, is an embroidered linen roll 70 metres (230 feet) long, and thought to have been made in England, very possibly in Canterbury. It records the Conquest of 1066, and its background (from the Norman viewpoint).

'One earl after another must rule the land, he who wishes his realm to prosper …'

From the Old English poem Widsith, *7th century*

DRAGON HEAD

Norman ships bore figureheads like the ships of their Viking ancestors. This is from the Gokstad ship, found near Oslo in 1880.

THE YEAR OF TWO INVASIONS

'I do not think it right that either my men or his [Harold's] should perish in conflict over a quarrel that is none of their making.'

William of Normandy, 1066, offering single combat as
an alternative to invasion

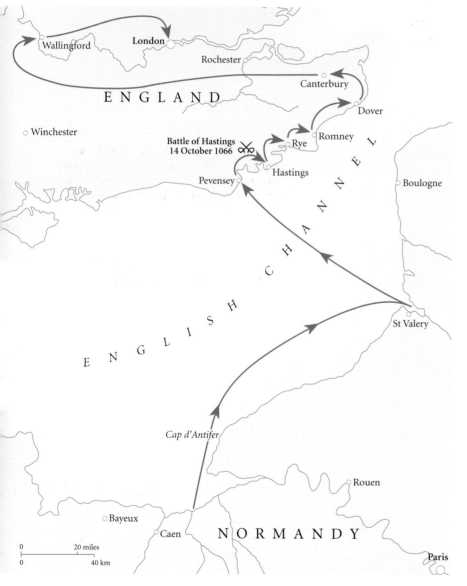

THE NORMAN INVASION

The Normans moved up from their home territory around Caen to cross the Channel at a narrower point. English naval forces were in the wrong place, guarding the Thames estuary and east coast.

IN NORMANDY, William gathered his army for invasion. His men built hundreds of ships, stockpiled weapons, rounded up horses and supplies, cut timber for prefabricated forts. The duke seemed confident, scoffing at counsellors who ventured to point out the hazards of crossing the sea to defeat the English on their own soil.

By July the ships were ready. Such preparations could not be made secretly and, alerted by reconnaissance, the English army was ready for the Normans. Then the wind changed, keeping William's ships in harbour in France. Not even he could command the weather. But those same winds carried a new challenger into the action, forcing Harold to face about and confront Hardrada's fleet sailing in from the North Sea. He also had a Godwin family problem to settle.

Harold's violent and unreliable brother, Tostig, was a thorn in his side. Party to a revolt in 1065, Tostig had been stripped of his lands and, as a vengeful outcast, took to piracy along the south coast before throwing in his lot with Harald Hardrada. Appearing off the east coast, the invading Norsemen, plus Tostig, sailed up the River Ouse to York, where they won a savage battle against the local English militia at Gate Fulford.

Harold was persuaded that the North Sea threat was more pressing than the one that faced him from the Channel. With characteristic speed, he gathered troops and marched north to Yorkshire. Just five days after the Norwegians' victory at Gate Fulford, the English army fell upon them at Stamford Bridge and – from the greatest battle in the 250-year history of Viking invasion – Harold emerged bloodily triumphant. By sunset at the end of a murderous day (25 September 1066), Hardrada, Tostig and most of the Norwegians lay dead. Over 300 ships had brought the Norse army to England; 34 were enough to carry the survivors home.

Harold's celebrations were short. Three days later, 700 Norman ships landed at Pevensey on the Sussex coast. Unwelcome as the news was, Harold was apparently confident that he could crush this second challenge. Without pausing to regroup his forces, the king dashed south to defend his heartland. Fresh soldiers were promised. Harold put his trust in speed and surprise.

NORMAN INVASION SHIPS

Norman ships, like those of the Vikings, were clinker-built, from overlapping planks of wood. They had square linen sails, carved animal heads on the prow and long oars at the stern for steering. The Conqueror's ship, *Mora*, may have carried a guiding lantern on its masthead, for others to follow at night or in fog. William's fleet waited six weeks for a favourable wind. Catching the evening tide on 27 September, it sailed to England in darkness, crossing in a few hours.

TIMBER FOR WILLIAM'S INVASION FLEET

Norman woodcutters fell trees to build William's fleet. Timber was also prepared for 'flat-pack' forts, while archers worked on their bows. Norman archers shot a bow shorter than the later medieval longbow but were (in William's opinion) much better than English bowmen.

FLAGSHIP'S FAIR WIND

William's ship, flying his banner, crosses the Channel, with shields slung along the gunwale. Note the steersman in the stern, with the big steering oar.

THE NORMAN SOLDIER

RA:AN GLORVM EX

IRON HEADGEAR

Both armies at Hastings wore helmets, made of iron like this one, or toughened leather. The iron helmet was worn over a padded headpiece.

HAROLD KNEW AND RESPECTED his enemy, after his experiences as William's reluctant ally in Normandy. But fighting on home ground, and buoyed up by their crushing victory over the Norwegians, Harold's troops were in good heart. The quick march south, however, sapped their energy. William's men were fresh.

Earlier invaders, such as the Romans, had landed troops unopposed and the Normans were equally lucky in 1066. The English fleet, out of position, could not prevent the Normans from beaching their ships and setting up a base camp. William, a commander of Roman efficiency, oversaw the unloading of men, armour,

supplies, fortification materials and horses. His invasion force was heavily armoured yet mobile, designed to crush, move on and crush again.

The two armies had different fighting styles. The Normans used many more horsemen, clad in chain-mail armour, with conical iron helmets and kite-shaped shields. The English strapped round or oval shields to their left arms. They wore mail coats, too, although the hastily gathered, locally levied troops who were summoned to Harold's banner probably wore little body protection. Archers could inflict heavy casualties on lightly armoured troops standing close together as was the Saxon custom.

MAILED CHARGERS

The Norman cavalryman wore a hauberk, a knee-length shirt of mail, and iron helmet. His kite-shaped shield was of leather, stretched on a wooden frame. In the charge he almost stood in the stirrups, using his lance to thrust at the enemy.

Where the Normans really scored was in their use of cavalry. Its mobility, added to the shock-value of the charge, gave them a huge advantage against the English, who tradition-ally fought on foot. Norman knights could smash through infantry, their lances opening gaps in the enemy line where they could wreak havoc with flailing swords and maces.

The English method of fighting – side by side, shield to shield – had changed little in centuries, and their battles were almost always bloody bouts of endurance and attrition. The king was pivotal, surrounded by his personal bodyguard, the housecarls, whose favoured weapon was the long-handled axe, swung two-handed to scythe through all in its path.

ANGLO-SAXON AXEMAN

An English housecarl, with his axe. Housecarls swished these fearsome weapons in a double-handed 'figure of eight'. They fought till they dropped in defence of their lord.

BOLD BOWMAN

A Norman archer, with short bow and a fistful of arrows.

'… loud and far resounded the bray of the horns; and the shock of the lances, the mighty strokes of maces, and the quick clashing of swords …'

Robert Wace, Norman chronicler, on 11th-century warfare

HASTINGS 1066

HORSED ARMOUR
William's cavalry charged repeatedly against the English line of men on foot.

IT HAS BEEN SAID that we know more about Hastings than any other medieval battle, such was its importance to contemporaries and to later generations. The English camped for the night of Friday 13 October, but were roused at daybreak by the sight of Normans advancing towards them. Saxon England fought for its life that autumn Saturday on Senlac Hill. Harold had chosen to fight a defensive battle, defending high ground astride the road to London and deploying his army along a 500-metre (550-yard) front. Each side had between 3,000 and 7,000 men, with the Normans having perhaps a slight advantage in numbers.

The Normans fanned out to attack the English line, their battle-cry *'Dex aie'* ('with God's aid') countered by the bellowed 'Out, out' of the English, each side taunting and defying the other. At first the heavily armoured Norman cavalry had difficulty crossing the marshland between the two armies, but the English were equally beset by arrows from the Norman archers.

The pattern was simple: Normans charged; the English stood their ground. The Bayeux Tapestry gives a dramatic tableau of the carnage – men and horses cut down by spears, swords, arrows and axes. William is said to have had three horses killed beneath him, and at one point is shown raising his helmet, to show wavering followers that he still lived.

STRIKING ENCOUNTER

Robert Wace, Norman chronicler, describing an encounter during the Battle of Hastings:

'The knight spurred and his horse carried him on well till he charged the Englishman, **striking him over the helmet so that it fell down over his eyes,** and as he stretched out his hand to raise it … the Norman cut off his right hand …'.

CARPET OF CORPSES
The frieze to the Bayeux Tapestry shows bodies of soldiers slain during the day-long battle.

'William came upon him unawares … but the king [Harold] fought against him with those men who would follow him, and there was great slaughter …' The Anglo-Saxon Chronicle *for 1066*

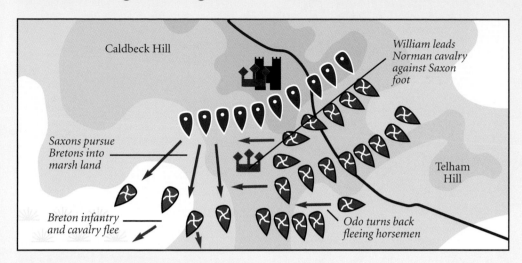

THE BATTLE OF HASTINGS AROUND NOON

The battle of Hastings, fought on 14 October on Senlac Hill (Battle in East Sussex), followed a familiar military story. It was a battle almost won through dogged resistance (the Saxon shield-wall defied the Norman cavalry) but finally lost by impetuosity as the Saxons broke ranks to pursue an apparently fleeing enemy and were overwhelmed. This map shows the situation halfway through the day-long battle.

The English fought as they had always done, on foot, behind locked shields, standing firm all morning against archers and cavalry. Then, about noon, Bretons on the Norman left recoiled in real or feigned disorder, and some of the English broke ranks in pursuit, weakening the shield-wall. Perhaps twice more the Normans feigned retreat, to entice more English from their hilltop. The Norman cavalry, however, still charged into the English, whose ranks were further weakened by hails of arrows. With the human wall breached, the fight centred on Harold's standard. The king himself was probably wounded in the eye (as shown in the Bayeux Tapestry), before being killed, along with his brothers Gurth and Leofwine. The royal bodyguard fought to the last man. Others fled, though some stayed to slaughter over-eager Norman pursuers as the October light failed.

Under cover of night, the survivors slipped away. The dead lay in heaps. William 'ate and drank among the dead and made his bed that night upon the field'. Harold's body, at first treated with contempt, was eventually buried at Waltham. After 500 years of Saxon rule in England, invading Normans ('Northmen') had finally taken the land.

67

HASTINGS CASTLE

The Bayeux Tapestry depicts events before and after the invasion. Here King William oversees the building of the castle at Hastings.

CROSSING POINT

A late 19th-century painting by Henry John Kinnaird of the River Thames at Wallingford, Oxfordshire, where William's army crossed, after encircling London. London Bridge had been held against him.

WILLIAM PAUSED, waiting for the submission of those English nobles left alive. No word came. He then marched east to Dover, where an outbreak of dysentery forced a week's delay. Ravaging Kent, he entered Canterbury, then swung west across the North Downs. Facing sporadic resistance as they circled London, the Normans sliced through Surrey and crossed the Thames. Now Archbishop Stigand submitted. They then tramped on

DESTRUCTIVE MARCH

The march of the Normans through England was marked by destruction, and long remembered – as this 15th-century illustration of ruined buildings shows.

through the Chilterns, receiving submission in December from the English earls in Hertfordshire. Reinforcements from Normandy took Winchester.

❧

With London secured, William was crowned King of England on Christmas Day, 1066. The ceremony was not without incident. Norman guards at Westminster Abbey mistook the shouts of acclaim for insurrection and set fire to surrounding houses. The ceremony continued, although the clergy were terrified and the king 'was trembling violently'.

> *'William, earl of Normandy, came into Pevensey and as soon as his men were ready to move, they built a castle at Hastings.'*
>
> The Anglo-Saxon Chronicle, *1066*

NORTHERN MUSCLE
Pickering Castle in Yorkshire is a Norman motte-and-bailey fortress. On top of an earth mound was the lord's stronghold. Around it was a walled enclosure. By 1100, there were at least 500 such castles across England.

The leaderless English still offered some resistance in the west, in Mercia and in Northumbria. Edric the Wild led an uprising in Herefordshire, while Harold's illegitimate sons staged an attempted counter-invasion from Ireland. The most serious challenge came in 1069, led by Edgar the Aetheling, prince of Wessex, in alliance with Sweyn of Denmark, whose fleet arrived off the north coast. It sparked fresh unrest across the country. William acted with typical ruthlessness. He took on the North personally, while his subordinates subdued the South and West. The Conqueror's 'harrying of the North' – a systematic scorching of rebel territory on both sides of the Pennines – passed into folklore: as the *Chronicle* puts it, 'he laid waste all the shire'. Nor was Viking England spared. York's Vikings had joined up with Hardrada, making William determined to crush them.

In 1069 the city was burned. The new king made few friends, but left few of his enemies with the will or means to fight. Already the Normans had begun to consolidate their conquest, by fortification, taking over ancient Roman forts, such as Pevensey in Sussex, and building new fortresses with awesome speed. One of two wooden castles in York is said to have taken only eight days to complete.

In this way, William's small army of occupation exerted an iron grip, which they extended rapidly through a chain of basic but effective wooden motte-and-bailey castles. An earth mound (the motte) was surrounded by a wooden palisade that formed an enclosure (the bailey), within which was the tower (the keep). Stone in time replaced wood as, in the 35 years following the Conquest, about 200 castles were built to subdue William's new realm.

SAXONS SUBDUED

THE NORMAN CASTLE served as barracks, watchtower, fort and administrative headquarters. Within a century, stone-built castles commanded the landscape, and from these symbols of Norman domination, cavalry patrols rode out to stifle uprisings and quell discontent.

Though cowed, the Saxons were not yet passive. Local hero Hereward the Wake fought a spirited guerrilla campaign from the Isle of Ely, joining forces with the Danes to attack Peterborough Abbey. By 1070, however, his Danish allies had wearied of the adventure and Hereward's resistance petered out.

There was one more flurry, in 1075; this time two Normans, the newly created Earls of Hereford and East Anglia, joined forces with the last of the English earls, Waltheof. Although they too sought Danish aid, the longships came too late to do anything but attack York, and the

WILLIAM'S CORONATION
This late medieval painting shows William being crowned King of England. Onlookers seem few and hardly rapturous.

insurgency was soon extinguished. Waltheof had his head cut off – having been betrayed by his wife (William's niece, and loyally Norman) who was duly rewarded with more land to soften the pangs of widowhood.

DOMESDAY BOOK
The Domesday Book was so named because, as on the last Day of Judgement (Doom), no one could escape its scrutiny. William was as thorough in assessing England as he had been in planning its conquest.

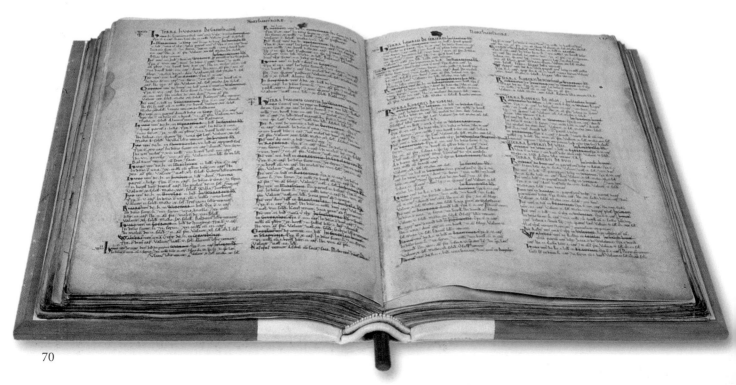

YORKSHIRE GRIT
Richmond's castle was a stony sign of the new Norman regime. This was one of the first northern towns to be 'Normanized'.

William set about ordering and evaluating his new kingdom. Chepstow Castle, built in 1070 by William FitzOsberne, was the first Norman castle constructed entirely of stone, soon to be followed by the great towers at Colchester and London. Norman castles were on a grand scale: Dover, for example, has 27 towers in its outer walls with 14 square towers on the inner ring. The Romans, first fortifiers of the Kent port, would have been impressed.

Steadily and remorselessly, the French-speaking Normans took over England's government and Church. English land was William's own battle spoil, shared out to the commanders who helped him win it. In return for his 'gift', each Norman lord swore allegiance to the king. This contract was the basis of Norman 'feudalism'. By the time William ordered the Domesday Book survey of his kingdom in 1086, some 200 Normans had replaced over 4,000 Saxon landlords.

William granted half of all farmland to the nobles, or barons, and a quarter to the Church. The rest he kept for himself. No castle could be built without the king's permission and no baron could keep a private army. But to counterbalance the barons' local powers, the king kept the Saxon system of sheriffs, to act on his behalf. He confirmed the laws of Edward the Confessor, and even tried to learn English, but by the end of William's reign the Norman flair for adaptation had produced an Anglo-French administration that was thoroughly 'Normanized'.

DOCUMENT NUMBER ONE

William's 'big idea' – the ultimate tax survey, the arbiter in every legal dispute over land – was the Domesday Book, made in 1086. Its two million words, written in Latin, list 13,418 place names. Domesday describes the main towns, landholders and manors belonging to William the Conqueror and his tenants and, as a picture of life in the 11th century, has no parallel in Europe.

NORMAN SWORDS
Straight and double-edged, the Norman sword was designed to be swung with two hands.

'He sent his men all over England …and had them find out … what or how much everybody had who was occupying land in England, in land or cattle, and how much money it was worth.'

Domesday, as reported in The Anglo-Saxon Chronicle

Scotland, Wales and Ireland

SCOTLAND DID NOT ESCAPE the Normans' attention for long. Malcolm Canmore had been king for eight years in 1066, and saw ways of turning England's conquest to his own advantage. Having once sought exile himself at the English court, he offered shelter from Norman rule to English refugees including Edgar the Aetheling and his sisters. Malcolm further incensed William by marrying, as his second wife, Margaret, one of the royal sisters.

William promptly invaded Scotland in 1072 to discourage any future support for Saxon rebels. Norman force worked: Malcolm agreed a truce, pledging loyalty to William as overlord, but the Scottish king remained a thorn in the Norman side, frequently violating his obligations by raiding across the border. Malcolm's wife Margaret brought an English flavour to the rough and ready Scottish court, and a reforming enthusiasm to the Scottish Church. Relations with the Norman regime in England remained tricky,

VIKINGS SEE THE LIGHT

St Magnus Cathedral in Kirkwall (11th-century) shows the influence of the Norwegian Vikings in the Orkney Islands. Viking rule there was consolidated by King Magnus III Barefoot in 1102.

ROYAL COUPLE

Malcolm Canmore was a nephew of Earl Siward of Northumbria, and well acquainted with English politics. Queen Margaret (his second wife) persuaded him to replace Gaelic with English at court. Of their six sons, three became kings of Scotland.

however, and by swearing an oath to the English king, Malcolm had offered a potentially dangerous hostage to fortune.

In 1087, William the Conqueror died from an injury sustained while besieging a town in defence of Normandy. He left the duchy to his eldest son Robert. England he left to William, called 'Rufus' (red) because of his florid complexion. The third son, Henry (later Henry I), was left a fortune in silver. As king, William Rufus fought to extend Norman rule into south Wales and secure his hold on northern England, where he refortified Carlisle, previously under Scottish control.

'The natives, from the constant warfare in which they engage … are bold and active. Skilful on horseback, quick on foot, not nice [fussy] as to their diet. By such men alone can their final conquest be accomplished …' Gerald of Wales (1147–1223), on the Norman efforts to conquer Wales and Ireland

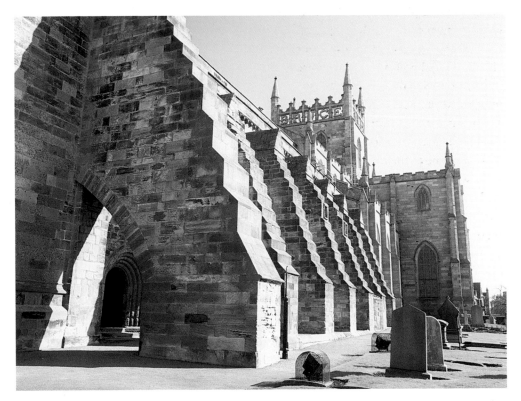

On his fifth raid across the border in 1093, King Malcolm was killed at Alnwick. The English king then nominated three sons of Malcolm (Duncan II, Edmund and Edgar) to the Scottish throne in turn, as his vassals.

In 1098 Edgar drove the Norwegian king Magnus Barelegs from the Scottish mainland, allowing Magnus and his heirs to remain 'lords of the isles'. The Western Isles remained Norse until 1266, while Orkney and Shetland became officially Scottish only in 1469, when they formed part of the marriage settlement between King James III and his Scandinavian bride, Margaret of Denmark.

Wales and Ireland also felt the weight of the Norman invaders. In the first ten years after the Conquest, William pressurized the Welsh border, granting land to powerful 'marcher' barons who then exploited any Welsh weakness to enlarge their estates further. So began two centuries of declining Welsh independence, culminating in the death of the last prince of Wales in 1282, during the wars against Edward I. Ireland was not invaded until 1169–70, when Henry II sanctioned an expedition led by Richard de Clare, Earl of Pembroke (known as 'Strongbow'). The kings of Ireland were forced to acknowledge Henry as their overlord, and Norman barons were granted Irish lands.

LIFE IN NORMAN BRITAIN

MOST PEOPLE IN NORMAN ENGLAND lived in the country, on the manor of a noble or churchman. According to the Domesday Book, the king held around 17 per cent of the land, bishops and abbots about 26 per cent, with 54 per cent shared by about 190 other large landholders: the barons. Barons let out their lands to knights and freemen, who in turn let land to the peasants who worked the lord's land and their own.

The Domesday survey reveals most English people as living from the land, sharing fields and cultivating small plots. Land was measured in hides (or carucates in Viking areas), roughly 60–120 acres, reckoned to be what an eight-oxen team could plough.

The majority of these people were not 'free' but tied by feudal obligations to the manor where they were born. Free peasants were most likely to live in the old Viking regions of eastern England. Villagers (villeins) living on

GREAT SNORING TITHE BARN
This Norfolk barn is a survivor of over 2,000 tithe barns built in England between 1066 and 1400.

RECKONING KETTERING

Domesday gives snapshots of local life in Norman England. The town of Kettering in Northamptonshire, for example, was recorded as having '… 10 hides [600 to 1200 acres] … and all the men render 50 hens and 640 eggs. **And besides this Ailric holds 13 acres with 2 acres of meadow, and pays for them 16 pence.** And there is a mill with a miller and it pays 20 shillings. And 8 cottars … work [for the lord] 1 day each week. And each of them gives 1 penny for a he-goat if he has one and 1 halfpenny for a nanny-goat.'

'The Isle … is most delightful for charming fields and pastures … remarkable for beasts of chase … fertile in flocks and herds. Its woods and vineyards are not worthy of equal praise.'

A French knight describes the Isle of Ely
to William I, around 1070

a lord's manor – on land (a 'fief') held on behalf of the king – worked their landlord's fields as well as their own rented farm plots. Smaller parcels of land were worked by the poorer smallholders (bordars) and cottagers (cottars). About 10 per cent of the population were slaves – though there were fewer slaves than before the Conquest.

From Domesday, we learn that sheep were plentiful, besides cows, oxen and horses. In 1086, Castle Hedingham in Essex had 100 goats, 160 sheep and 100 pigs. Grazing animals were usually left to forage for themselves. Goats supplied milk, pigs rooted for nuts in woodland, and farmers harvested crops of wheat, oats, barley and beans. Domesday lists 6,000 watermills, many with eel traps which supplied a good source of food and revenue. Ely teemed with eels – hence the name. Life was as hard as it had always been. But there were a few perks: a cowherd got milk for a week after an old cow calved; a shepherd got 12 nights' dung (for fuel) at Christmas and one lamb in spring, while the 'woodward' got every tree that blew down in a gale.

PEASANT DIGGERS

The peasants worked with wooden spades tipped with iron; their work was grindingly hard, year in, year out.

SHEPHERDS AND SHEEP

A pre-Conquest Saxon painting shows a peaceful scene. As life settled down after the Conquest, most people sought normality and a full stomach, whoever wore the crown.

75

CHURCH AND TOWN

SOLIDITY AND GRACE

Norman churches are just as imposing as Norman castles: Gloucester, Durham and Ely, for example. William of St Carileph, the bishop appointed by William the Conqueror to Durham, oversaw the start of work on the Norman cathedral (above) in 1093. Its rib vaulting – the earliest in Europe – seems to soar towards heaven.

THE NORMAN CHURCH was a ship of state as well as a saver of souls. It held much of the conquered land (Bishop Odo, William's half- brother, had land in 22 English counties), and provided clerical manpower, including the scribes and commissioners who created the Domesday Book. The priest was the foremost resident of a Norman village – the survey mentions a thousand or so priests, but there were undoubtedly many more. Some churchmen lived comfortably, receiving a tithe (tenth) payment in goods or money from their parishioners. Other priests were very poor, and had to take their share of the manor's manual labour.

King William had imprisoned the English archbishop Stigand in 1070, accusing him of being covetous and worldly.

Stigand's replacement at Canterbury was Lanfranc, a gifted Italian who brought the English Church much closer to the practices of Rome. The only English bishop to keep his job after 1066 was Wulfstan, the saintly Benedictine monk who rebuilt Worcester Cathedral, helped compile the Domesday Book and ended the capture and sale of slaves at Bristol. When Durham Cathedral was begun in 1093, William had already imported Benedictine monks to replace the Anglo-Saxon monastic community to which St Cuthbert had belonged some 400 years earlier.

Norman England had few towns, and those that did exist were small; only 18 had more than 2,000 inhabitants. Old ways persisted: Nottingham had two boroughs, one Saxon, one Norman, for 200 years after the Conquest. Norwich, with perhaps 5,000 people at the Conquest and over 2,000 sheep grazing around it, owed its wealth to wool. Local industries profited other towns too: iron-working at Corby (Northamptonshire), lead mining in the Dales at Matlock (Derbyshire), salt-panning at Droitwich

WINCHESTER INITIAL

An illuminated letter from the Winchester Bible, made for the Bishop of Winchester in the 12th century.

(Worcestershire). London's importance, as England's capital, grew steadily.

Town markets buttressed local prosperity but like the shops of modern times could suffer terminal downturns or even unfair competition. At Thetford, the Domesday Book records forlornly that '... in this manor there used to be a market on Saturdays. But William Malet [a Norman] ... made his castle at Eye, and he made another market ...'.

WARM WORK

Idlers warm themselves while the blacksmith plies his trade. Smiths were usually respected, other traders suspected of law-breaking. In Huntingdon, the fine for giving 'false measure' was fourpence, while any brewer making bad beer could be tipped into malodorous punishment on the 'dung stool'.

WINNER TAKES ALL

NORMAN VICTORY IN 1066 swept away the English nobility, who were either killed, exiled or deprived of their lands. Earldoms no longer carried the old Saxon political clout; in England power had shifted to the king, though Scottish earls retained their influence longer. Change affected every level of society. After the Conquest, for example, cash payment for rents grew more common, rather than rent paid in kind (goods and services). In northern England, land values fell by about a quarter between 1066 and 1086, evidence perhaps of William's savage campaigns there.

William's successors secured his conquest, notably Henry I, ablest of his sons and the only one born in England. Henry was ruthless, beating his eldest brother Robert to the crown as he was hastening home from the Holy Land, and later locking him up for life. But Henry did much to meld Norman and Saxon into a united people, with Welsh and Scottish kings remaining his 'vassals' (owing him loyalty).

Promising good government, he issued a charter of liberties and extended the administrative reforms begun by his father. Continuing Norman support for monastic reform, Henry received Cistercian monks to England, where they founded Rievaulx and Fountains abbeys in Yorkshire and raised sheep – England's medieval prosperity would be built on the wool trade.

The Norman dynasty managed to survive civil war in the early 1100s between Henry I's daughter Matilda and his nephew Stephen, by merging – in the person of Matilda's son Henry II (reigned 1154–89) – into the Plantagenet (or Angevin) line. Henry II ruled an empire larger than any English king before him – including England, Wales, Ireland, Anjou, Normandy, Brittany and Aquitaine. Saxon and Norman continued to fuse, to form a new kind of English, and to create a new landscape.

SPOILED BY VICTORY

Robert, Count of Mortain, another half-brother of the Conqueror, fought at Hastings. His reward was to be granted more land in England than any other Norman – except the king himself.

The Normans took over a country with perhaps between 1 and 2 million people (less than half the 4 to 5 million thought to have lived in Roman Britain). Their conquest left England, and ultimately the rest of Britain, an enduring legacy of language, law and architecture. The Normans gave fresh energy to the Saxon state, adapting law, government, Church and economy to create an efficient administration. They built massive castles and soaring cathedrals. They introduced over half the words we use in our language. They kept later invaders at bay and drew internal borders that still exist. Above all, William's victory at Hastings wrenched England away from the Scandinavian world and into the mainstream of European affairs.

AT THE HEAD OF A LINE

William I heads the line of Norman kings in this illustration from the Chronicle of England (c.1307–27) by Peter de Langtoft, written in Latin and French (not English), and now in the British Library.

ROCHESTER CASTLE

The abiding impression is of a mighty force allied to an implacable will: such was William the Conqueror's legacy. Grim fortresses such as Rochester in Kent could not be ignored by the people he and his descendants ruled.

79

INVASION FEARS AND SCARES

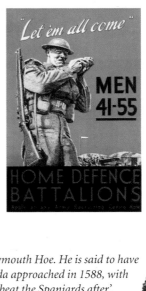

FEAR OF INVASION remained an ever-present political reality over the centuries. The Norman Conquest was the last full-scale successful invasion in Britain by a foreign power. However, as time passed many more minor incursions and cross-border adventures, besides fears and scares of threatened attack, convinced its people that Britain was either peculiarly blessed or fortunate to be an island.

During the wars later in the Middle Ages, castle architecture reached a golden age, particularly in the 14 great fortresses built by England's Edward I (reigned 1272–1307) in Wales. Smaller forts dotting the landscape from Scotland to the Scilly Isles also testify to the uncertainty and cost of medieval power politics. Edward I and Edward III waged war in Scotland until the Scots reasserted their independence at Bannockburn in 1314. Scotland remained a potential flashpoint, though, even after the union of crowns took place under King James VI (James I of England) in 1603. The Jacobite rising of 1745–46 was the last serious attempt at regime change, and it began, and ended, in Scotland.

For some 500 years, France and Spain were seen as the chief external threats to England, requiring a powerful navy and

NELSON'S FLAGSHIP

HMS Victory, still officially part of the Fleet, fought at Trafalgar in 1805. The famous ship is now in dry dock at Portsmouth.

CALL TO ARMS

The Home Guard was raised in 1940, as men past call-up age rallied to the cause of national defence.

FIRST THINGS FIRST

The statue of Sir Francis Drake on Plymouth Hoe. He is said to have finished a game of bowls as the Armada approached in 1588, with the remark 'There's time for that and beat the Spaniards after'.

coastal defences to be maintained against possible invasion. Yet these could be bypassed by ambitious usurpers and rebels slipping in and out of the country, to pursue what were often lost causes. Grander schemes came to nothing: the Spanish Armada of 1588, the Duke of Monmouth's invasion of 1685, Napoleon's plans for a cross-Channel assault in 1804.

The sea, and the navy, proved an effective deterrent to most invaders, although Britain was still building coastal forts in the mid 19th century. A new threat was posed by the advent of air power in the 20th century. In 1940, church bells might once more have rung to warn of enemy invasion, but for the heroism of Battle of Britain pilots. Falling bombs caused more damage than any invasion army in Britain's history ever did, but the islands' defences – ancient and modern – in the end held fast against a new enemy.

UNEASY LIES THE HEAD

SOME ANCIENT DEFENCES pre-dated the Normans: the English south coast Cinque Ports (Hastings, New Romney, Hythe, Dover and Sandwich) enjoyed privileges granted by Edward the Confessor (reigned 1042–66), in return for supplying men and ships. To the original five Cinque Ports, Richard I added Winchelsea and Rye, while other towns, such as Margate, had special status as link-ports in a defensive chain.

Such coastal defences were to scare off pirates, raiders and invaders, whether Norwegians, French, Scots or any other hostile neighbour. They were useful too in deterring usurpers and rebels. Medieval mini-invasions were frequently inspired by regal feuds. In 1326, Queen Isabella with her lover Roger Mortimer landed in England from France to depose her husband Edward II, while in 1399 Henry Bolingbroke returned from exile to oust Richard II and take the crown as Henry IV. Sometimes the ships and claimants went in the other direction: Henry V invaded France in 1415, to assert his right to the French crown. The Wars of the Roses saw frequent cross-Channel escapes and returns as the tide of civil war ebbed and flowed. They culminated in Henry Tudor's landing at Milford Haven in 1485, to defeat Richard III at Bosworth Field and make himself king, as Henry VII.

This first Tudor king of England kept a firm grip on the crown he had picked up at Bosworth, facing challenges from two 'pretenders': Lambert Simnel in 1487 and Perkin Warbeck in 1497. His wariness passed to his son Henry VIII who, despite the English victory at Flodden (1514) against 30,000 invading Scots, still feared seaborne attack, building new coastal forts

TUDOR TURRETS

Henry VIII's coastal castles such as that at St Mawes in Cornwall were advanced for their time, designed as gun-forts to blast enemy ships and serve as rallying points should invasion troops manage to land.

CANNON AT DEAL

Deal Castle in Kent is the largest of the coastal gun-forts constructed in under two years (1539–40) for King Henry VIII's wars.

MAKING WAVES

Edward IV of England invaded France in 1475. Here he is about to land for what turned out to be a fund-raising tour. The French paid up for the English to go home.

armed with cannon to keep off the French. Henry also embarked on an intensive naval rearmament programme, upgrading his father's warships and building new vessels.

Further symbolizing Henry's new confidence (or apprehension) was the 700-tonne *Mary Rose* (built 1509–11), which after a successful career was rebuilt in 1536 with new bronze cannon. Evidently dangerously top-heavy when crammed with heavily armed fighting men, *Mary Rose* sank in 1545 during a skirmish with the French off Portsmouth. New, more nimble ships succeeded her – and were soon needed in action, for in 1588 Henry's daughter Elizabeth I faced a mighty invasion force inspired by a foreign monarch's religious zeal – the Spanish Armada.

LANDLORD OR WARLORD?

Henry VII took steps to safeguard his throne by any means, including crafty taxation of potential enemies. In 1507 George Neville, Lord Burgavenny, was accused of having an illegal private army. Pleading guilty, he was fined £70,650 – an enormous sum. The noble lord's 'army' consisted of 471 hired men: 25 gentlemen, 4 priests, 440 yeomen [farmers] a cobbler and a tinker. Henry calculated the fine at the rate of £5 a man for 30 months!

THE ARMADA FOILED

ELIZABETH I WAS at constant risk from plotters seeking to overthrow her and return England to the bosom of the Catholic Church. It was a dream that obsessed Philip II of Spain, who was infuriated too by the piratical activities of the Virgin Queen's sea-captains: Hawkins, Frobisher, Drake and their fellow 'sea-dogs'.

In 1586 Philip ordered an invasion of England. An Armada of Spain's finest ships was to sail up the Channel to Calais, and there pick up a Spanish army from the Low Countries. Francis Drake's daring attack on Cadiz in 1587 delayed the fleet's departure, and early in 1588 the Armada's chosen admiral, Santa Cruz, died. His replacement, the Duke of Medina Sidonia, was no sailor, but the Armada that left Lisbon in July 1588 – 130 huge ships carrying 30,000 men and 2,500 cannon – seemed unequalled and invincible.

Against this juggernaut, the English mustered 197 craft under the command of Lord Howard of Effingham. His fleet had only half the manpower of the Spaniards, but his captains knew their coastline and its tides. Spanish seamen might be tough and experienced, yet their huge galleons were slower than most of the English ships, whose seamen were also capable of much faster gunnery.

First sight of the Armada was off the Scilly Isles. Warning beacons blazed along the south coast as the ships moved west in a crescent, harried by the English who had put out from Plymouth. But the Spanish were unable to draw their opponents into a close-quarters battle. On 6 August the fleet reached Calais, where the Duke of Parma's troops had yet to board their invasion barges. Hastily breaking off last-minute peace talks there, English

> *'For strength, assurance, nimbleness and swiftness of sailing, there are no vessels in the world to be compared with ours …'*
>
> *William Harrison,* Description of England, *1587*

BLOWN TO DESTRUCTION
This map shows the Armada's approach, close encounters, and disaster-strewn escape route.

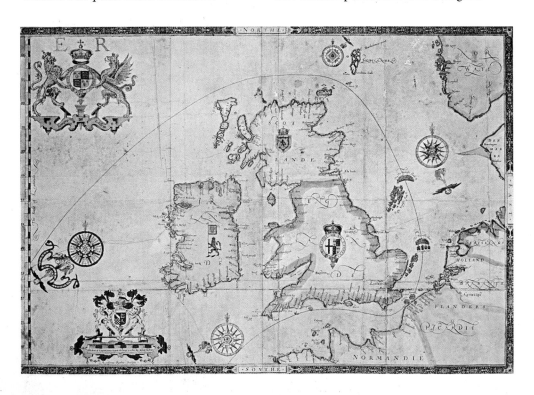

diplomats sent urgent messages that the enemy at anchor was open to attack. Fireships launched to drift on the tide among the Armada galleons caused much alarm but no real damage. The next day (8 August) some 70 ships fought an action off Gravelines in France. Only one Spanish ship was sunk but 1,400 Spaniards were killed or injured in the encounter by English cannon fire.

∽

Dawn found the Armada blown out to sea, northwards, with little option but to head for home, around Britain. On 18 August, when Elizabeth rallied her army at Tilbury with stirring words of defiance, the threat had passed. Medina Sidonia's flagship struggled back to Spain on 21 September. Fewer than half his 130 ships had survived and more than 10,000 men perished off, and on, the cold, grey, rock-strewn shores of Scotland and Ireland. The English, with not one ship lost, celebrated. Providence was obviously on their side. Had not God sent a wind to scatter Albion's foes?

FIERY WARNING

Beacons were lit along the south coast to warn of the Armada's approach, and to alert local militias.

ALL AT SEA

The Armada captains sought a close encounter, where the size and manpower of their great galleons made boarding the enemy a winning strategy. The English kept at long range, using their sailing superiority and sniping with their cannon.

PLOTS AND PRETENDERS

THE UNION OF CROWNS in 1603, when Scotland's King James VI became Britain's King James I, did not bring national harmony. Religious quarrels were the main source of trouble. The 1605 Gunpowder Plot was aimed at removing Protestant James and, with foreign help, replacing him with a Catholic princess. But the plotting was bungled, and there is little evidence of popular support. Fear and dislike of foreign intervention usually outweighed religious differences, except when the king was universally disliked. No foreign invader managed to take advantage of the English Civil War, which removed Charles I in 1649.

A foreign king, however, was sought after James II succeeded his brother Charles II in 1685. Humourless and stubborn, the Catholic James faced rebellions in Scotland by the Duke of Argyll, and in England by James Scott, Duke of Monmouth. Monmouth, an illegitimate son of Charles II, landed at Lyme in Dorset with an army raised in the Netherlands, hoping to make himself king. But defeat at the Battle of Sedgemoor, in Somerset, sank his cause and he was executed.

When James's wife produced a son in June 1688, fear of a Catholic dynasty overcame fear of a foreign invader. The king's Protestant son-in-law, William of Orange, landed unopposed in November 1688, and so began the brief and largely bloodless Glorious Revolution which carried William and Mary to the throne. James attempted a comeback via Ireland, but defeat at the Battle of the Boyne in 1690 finally sent him packing.

HOPELESS CAUSE
Rebel without a hope: James, Duke of Monmouth (1649–85), whose short-lived invasion collapsed at Sedgemoor.

ORDER FROM DISORDER
William of Orange landed at Torbay in Devon in 1688, to send James II hurrying into exile in France. Here William's army assembles amid the inevitable confusion of invasion.

The Jacobites' hopes died finally at Culloden as exhausted Highlanders were cut down by Redcoat artillery and bayonets. The battle was over in just 25 blood-soaked minutes.

For the next 50 years or so, plots and invasion rumours abounded. After the Act of Union (1707) that united the governments of England and Scotland, supporters of the ousted Stuarts, known as Jacobites, still plotted in France to put James II's son, James Edward Stuart, on the throne. Their plans were dashed when George I, grandson of Charles I's sister, arrived from Germany in 1714 to inaugurate the Hanoverian dynasty. A half-hearted 1715 invasion, backed by a Scottish clan uprising, fizzled out within three months, and James Edward Stuart retired to France.

Jacobites regrouped behind his son, the 'Young Pretender' Charles Edward Stuart. 'Bonnie Prince Charlie' landed in the Hebrides on 23 July 1745, rallying 1,200 men to his standard. 'The worst thing that can happen to me is to die at the head of such brave people as I find here,' he wrote to his father. A month later he marched into Edinburgh. The Jacobite army, swollen after a victory at Prestonpans on 21 September, crossed the border, taking Carlisle on 1 November. By 28 November Charles was dining in Manchester, on 4 December in Derby, and in London there was panic. At this point the Scots dithered: men were tired, their commanders divided. No English support had been forthcoming, and King George's army, led by the Duke of Cumberland, was advancing to do battle.

To Charles's dismay, the Scots turned homeward. On 16 April 1746, 6,000 Highlanders were butchered on Culloden Moor near Inverness by 9,000 Redcoats armed with artillery. After this, the last battle fought on British soil, Charles hid as a fugitive. On 20 September 1746 he left Scotland for France, never to return.

PRINCE'S FAREWELL

Flora Macdonald helped Bonnie Prince Charlie escape after Culloden. These were his parting words to her in Portree, Skye, June 1746: **'For all that has happened, I hope, Madam, we shall meet at St James's yet, and I will reward you there for what you have done.'** Eleven days later, Flora was arrested. Released in 1747, she later married and emigrated to America, but returned to Scotland to die, in 1790.

RULING THE WAVES

IF NOT BY SEA ....

... then by air, using the newly invented balloon. This whimsical picture shows Napoleon's troops crossing the Channel out of reach of the British Navy.

FRANCE, HAD BEEN Britain's rival on the world stage throughout the 18th century. When the American colonists rebelled against Britain in 1775, it was natural that France should side with the Americans. Among the embarrassments of this conflict was the occasion in 1778 when John Paul Jones, the Scot-turned-American sailor, had the temerity to land at Whitehaven, Cumbria. The war also motivated perhaps the smallest invasion in British history, a French attack on Jersey carried out in 1781.

In 1789 the French Revolution sent fresh shivers through the British establishment. New France was eager to continue the old warfare, despite the Royal Navy.

On 22 February 1797, 1,400 French troops landed at Fishguard in Wales, only to surrender in drunken disarray two days later to a British force half their number. In 1798, another French unit landed in Ireland to support Irish nationalists but, after winning a skirmish at Castlebar, was mopped up without much ado.

'Let us be masters of the Channel for six hours and we are masters of the world.'   *Napoleon Bonaparte, writing on 2 July 1804*

TRAFALGAR

This painting by Thomas Luny shows the scene around 3 o'clock in the afternoon, some two hours after Nelson was shot on the quarter-deck of HMS Victory.

By 1804, France had exchanged revolution for empire, under Napoleon Bonaparte. Thanks to his military genius – and the incompetence of his enemies – he had gained control of much of Europe. Britain, however, remained hostile to the new Europe, and so Napoleon ordered invasion preparations. His plan was to use barges to cross the Channel, land 150,000 troops with horses and guns, and capture London within five days – provided the French and Spanish fleets could sweep the Channel free of British warships. The 'nation of shopkeepers', as Napoleon called the English, put their trust in their navy, but also hurriedly erected a chain of stout, brick-built Martello towers (named after a tower on Corsica) at places where the French might land. In the event, the forts were not required. Napoleon's invasion barges never left France. British warships mounted a blockade of French ports and when the Franco-Spanish fleet attempted a breakout, it was tracked across the Atlantic Ocean and back again by Admiral Horatio Nelson, who finally brought it to battle at Cape Trafalgar on 21 October 1805.

The French and Spanish fleet was slightly bigger, at 33 ships to 27, and the fight fierce, but with 20 ships captured and 14,000 enemy dead to 1,587 British, the dying Nelson had his victory. Trafalgar had crossed seaborne invasion off Napoleon's agenda, leaving British control of the seas unshaken for a hundred years.

I CAN SEE YOU …
Napoleon (mocked by the cartoonist) and John Bull confront one another from opposite sides of the Channel in 1804.

ASSAULT ON JERSEY

On the night of 5/6 January 1781, a group of 800 or so French troops led by Baron de Rullecourt landed on Jersey in a bid to seize the island. The small British garrison, commanded by Major Francis Peirson, fought a brief engagement in St Helier's Royal Square which cost the lives of both commanders. The French survivors were transported to rotting hulks (prison ships), as prisoners of war.

'Never, in the field
of human conflict,
was so much owed
by so many to
so few.'

*Prime Minister
Winston Churchill,
of the pilots who fought in
the Battle of Britain, 1940*

CLEAN FOR ACTION

*A Home Guard volunteer cleans
his gun, while his wife increases
sock reserves.*

FLIGHT OF THE FEW

*Pilots dashing to their Spitfires
to take off from bumpy grass
fields – one of the enduring
images of the 1939–45 war.*

VICTORY AT TRAFALGAR did not end British
nervousness about sea invasion throughout the 19th century, though no serious
threat ever came to pass. Coastal forts,
such as those in the Solent, at Newhaven in
Sussex and at Crownhill, Plymouth, never
fired their guns in anger against ironclad
battleships. Only when German airships
appeared in the skies during the First
World War (1914–18) did a new, more
deadly threat materialize. Britain was now
open to attack from the air.

When the Second World War began in
September 1939, defence planners were
quickly made aware that warfare had
changed. The German air force had gained
overpowering air superiority, allowing
ground forces to storm through Poland,
Norway, Belgium, the Netherlands and
France. By May 1940 the British had to
evacuate 338,000 troops from Dunkirk.
Britain's last line of defence was the
narrow strip of water separating it from
Nazi-occupied Europe.

> *'We shall defend our island, whatever the cost may be. We shall fight on the beaches, we shall fight on the landing grounds, we shall fight in the fields and in the streets, we shall fight in the hills; we shall never surrender.'*
>
> *Winston Churchill, speaking to the House of Commons, 4 June 1940*

That summer, Britain prepared to fight off Hitler's invasion, code-named Operation Sealion. Beaches were strewn with barbed wire and tank traps; concrete pill-boxes and machine-gun posts sprouted in fields and streets; trenches were dug; roadblocks set up. Route-signs disappeared from roads patrolled by men of the Home Guard (some in their 80s) carrying an assortment of weapons of varying vintages. Observers watched and listened for enemy aircraft, expecting paratroop drops to precede any amphibious assault by the German army. While Churchill promised a fight to the death, secret plans were put in place to evacuate the King and Queen to Canada, set up a government in exile, and organize resistance and sabotage at home.

The Germans knew that to gain air superiority they must destroy the Royal Air Force. Only then could *Luftwaffe* planes drive the Royal Navy from the Channel and shield the invasion craft. Hitler and *Luftwaffe* chief Goering thought five days would complete the task. The Nazi regime hoped that the British would see reason and make peace, despite Churchill's vow to fight on beaches and in fields. And so in August 1940 began the Battle of Britain.

ONE THAT WON'T GO HOME

A defiant Tommy in full kit stands guard over a shot-down German Me 109 fighter during the dark days and nights of 1940 – 41.

Though outnumbered, the RAF's Hurricane and Spitfire fighters were highly effective, while radar gave vital early warning of incoming raiders. German failure to destroy fighter bases and radar stations proved crucial. By the end of August, Hitler's thoughts had turned away from invasion and on 7 September *Luftwaffe* pilots instead turned their attention to bombing London: the Blitz had begun. Blackout, bombsites, barrage balloons, anti-aircraft guns and air-raid shelters soon became only too familiar all over Britain. Death and danger remained daily threats, but after the summer sky-battles of 1940, the invasion menace had receded. On 12 October Hitler cancelled Operation Sealion. Germany had suffered its first setback; Britain fought on.

NO BATHING, BY ORDER

The seafront at Eastbourne, in Sussex, in the summer of 1940. Anti-invasion defences replaced buckets and spades.

THE LEGACY OF INVASION

CELTIC HERITAGE

Celtic artists could imbue even a belt buckle with vigorous life, a tradition which their modern counterparts have preserved.

YORK MINSTER

There has been a Christian church on the Minster site since Roman times; in the floor of the crypt is the base of a pillar from the courtyard of the Roman legionary fortress. Here, in AD 306, Constantine was proclaimed emperor.

IN EVERY PART OF BRITAIN is the evidence of our ancestors, who named the rivers, the mountains, the towns and villages, even the streets and fields. Language is one of the most fascinating trails left by successive settlers and invaders. Each cultural scene-shift added new riches and subtleties. Some of the oldest surviving names in Britain are those of rivers, names given long before the Romans invaded: England has several Avons, Stours and Calders because many Celtic names for rivers simply mean 'water'. The more hilly and wooded the landscape, the more Celtic place names are likely to be found. In the north and east, Norse names crop up, such as *fell*, meaning mountain and *dale*, meaning valley.

Celtic culture survived the Roman conquest in places where Romans chose not to tread – in Ireland, for example – or where their footfall was fleeting – in Scotland and the wilds of the west. It was also kept alive in the Christian monasteries after the Romans left, creating the rich and literate artistic civilization that produced the Book of Kells and the Lindisfarne Gospels. Celtic myth and history lived on in the story cycles of Wales (such as the *Mabinogion*) and of Ireland. So too did the bardic tradition, in the form of the Welsh eisteddfod.

Language endures, changed and enriched by new words and concepts, while architecture crumbles or is recycled. For the past two thousand years, old buildings have given way to new. The Romans gave Britain its first real towns, many still important today. They made London the chief city of the land. At Dover, they built Britain's first lighthouse. They laid our first all-weather roads, spearing straight across country. As well as introducing such urban refinements as public baths, theatres and sports arenas, the Romans were also the first serious gardeners in Britain, bringing in an assortment of new food-plants including carrots, peas, asparagus, lettuce, radishes and turnips.

The Saxons and Vikings brought a vigorous oral tradition of their own, one rich in mythology and heroic tales that echo down the ages from *Beowulf* to *The Lord of the Rings*. Old English, the language evolving from the tongues of the Angles, Saxons, Jutes and others, gave us everyday words such as house, mother, bread, water. Wine and butter were borrowed from Latin. Pig is from Old English, pork and bacon are Norman-French; cow and deer are English, beef and venison are French. Breakfast is English, while dinner and supper are French. When one Norman baron moved into Yorkshire, he gave his castle a French name 'Richmond', while another castle on the River Aire near a tumbledown bridge became Pontefract – 'the bridge that is broken'.

Roman towns had crumbled by the time the Normans came. Saxon churches, most of them built of wood, were replaced by Norman stone. Roman Britain survives in impressive fragments, such as the Roman baths at Bath; the legionary fort at Caerleon; the villas at Chedworth and Lullingstone; the 'palace' at Fishbourne; and Hadrian's Wall. Many ancient sites reveal ongoing use and adaptation over the years. Pevensey Castle, a Roman fort, was used by the Saxons and has a Norman castle in one corner.

Britons, Romans, Picts, Scots, Angles, Saxons, Jutes, Vikings, Normans: all contributed to the slow, and at times, painful evolution of a united kingdom, a country of nations. Among their legacies was a mercantile adventuring spirit, a taste for adventure, exploration and colonization. While the Saxons were inspired by loyalty to a leader, Vikings imported a Scandinavian belief in the value of popular consent, a basic form of democracy. To this, the Normans added efficient bureaucracy, an attention to detail seen at its most spectacular in the Domesday Book.

EDINBURGH CASTLE

Castle Rock has been a fortress since the 500s. From the Gaelic Dun-eideann ('hill of Eidin'), Edinburgh was once held by the Angles and became a Scottish royal stronghold in the reign of Malcolm Canmore (1058–93).

SAXON CROSS

The Winster Moor gold and garnet cross, from Derbyshire. It was made around AD 700, when Christianity was still a new faith among the English.

LONDON WALL

A vestige of Roman London's wall survives in the heart of the city. It was the Romans who built London's first bridge and made the city a centre for trade and administration.

THE DOMESDAY BOOK

Perhaps the best thing the Normans left – a priceless historical record of medieval life, compiled by one man writing by hand up to 3,500 words a day. It is now in the National Archives at Kew, in London.

The Domesday survey is a legacy greater even than castles and cathedrals, longer lasting than the forts and coastal defences that still stand around Britain's shores as witnesses to centuries of triumphs and disasters.

To the English of 1086, the Domesday survey was a symbol of defeat and oppression – conquest by pen as well as sword. Yet by the 1300s, the same survey meant hope for a peasant seeking to escape from the tied labour demanded by a landlord. Domesday represents a continuity of history unique in Europe. To be mentioned in Domesday grants the ultimate historical status to the 13,418 places listed in the book, whether their subsequent fate was to boom and grow, or to stagnate and shrink.

Very few of those Domesday places vanished altogether. Like the people who were invaded, or who came as invaders and settlers, they learned to survive and adapt. Like all the contributions of all the invaders in Britain, Domesday provided a fresh foundation for growth, enriched by and drawing from what had existed before.

CABINET WAR ROOMS

Visitors can now see inside the rooms, deep beneath Whitehall, where Winston Churchill and his colleagues plotted the defence of Britain in 1940.

MODERN VIKINGS

Every year as part of the Jorvik Viking Festival, enthusiasts re-enact the Vikings' capture of the city of York in 866.

INDEX